10-MINUTE IDEAS FOR EARLY YEARS

Counting fun

Helen Elis Jones

■ **Quick activities for any time of the day**

■ **Links to Early Learning Goals** ■ **Time-saving photocopiables**

Credits

Author
Helen Elis Jones

Editor
Victoria Lee

Assistant Editor
Kate Element

Series Designer
Anna Oliwa

Designer
Andrea Lewis

Cover Illustration
Craig Cameron/Art
Collection

Illustrations
Debbie Clark

Text © 2004
© 2004 Scholastic Ltd

Designed using Adobe InDesign

Published by Scholastic Ltd
Villiers House
Clarendon Avenue
Leamington Spa
Warwickshire
CV32 5PR

www.scholastic.co.uk

Printed by Bell & Bain

1 2 3 4 5 6 7 8 9   4 5 6 7 8 9 0 1 2 3

British Library Cataloguing-in-Publication Data
A catalogue record for this book is available from the British Library.

ISBN 0-439-97095-4

Contents

Contents

Measures

Shape and space

Photocopiables

Introduction

This book is one of a series that provides the early years practitioner with a range of simple, practical activities covering all six Areas of Learning encompassed in the Early Learning Goals. *Counting Fun* focuses on Mathematical Development. Each activity will have a duration of about ten minutes and will require little or no preparation. There are 60 main activity ideas presented in an easy-to-use format and 14 photocopiable sheets, all of which are aimed at four-year-old children with support and extension ideas for three- to five-year-olds.

Most aspects of daily life, both within and outside the teaching situation, include elements of counting. We count the number of steps on the stairs, the number of letters in our name, plates when laying the table, and so on. The importance of counting is emphasised in the official documentation regarding teaching and learning mathematics to pupils under five and Key Stage 1. It also features strongly in the mental starter of the three-part mathematics lesson as advocated in the *National Numeracy Strategy.*

But how can we assist children to count and to recognise the sequence of numbers? It's so easy for practitioners to forget the difficulties involved with remembering the 'number rhyme', as it is so familiar to us. Perhaps learning to count in a different language and perhaps mixing up the word order would help us appreciate the children's difficulties!

There is no best way of teaching children to count. Children respond differently to experiences, and what works for one may not work for another. To help children become confident in the counting process they need a broad range of experiences, some of which could appeal to their different senses, such as sight, hearing, touching, speaking or even shouting! These practical ideas will help the children to memorise the counting system, and ensure that everyone, practitioners and children, enjoys counting in the classroom.

This book is full of activities to support and develop the children's learning. They will help children to count up to ten everyday objects, to recognise the number sequence 0 to 10, to compare two numbers or sets of objects and, more importantly, to gain pleasure and confidence in using numbers and to begin to understand what they represent in different contexts.

This book is divided into six chapters:
- Numbers as labels and for counting
- Numbers as sets
- Rhymes and stories
- Patterns and structures
- Measures
- Shape and space.

The range of activities included within each chapter can be adapted to suit the individual needs and abilities of the children in your care. The aim of the book is not to teach the children to count to ten by rote, but to provide them with a wide range of interesting activities, based at a similar level, which will help them to understand number concepts through active participation.

Activities can be repeated and adapted to further reinforce the children's number skills. Language skills also need to be fostered through the use of correct terminology and by ensuring the children have as many opportunities as possible to use and practise words and phrases.

Using the photocopiable sheets

There are 14 photocopiable sheets provided with the book. These can be employed to further develop certain activities or used as an extra resource on their own. References to their use are indicated within the activities themselves. These sheets include a rhyme poster, a folding star and a variety of simple games, all of which the practitioner can photocopy as required for the children in their setting.

Resources

Children, especially at this young age, benefit from using practical resources. These can help illustrate mathematical aspects and can provide a model for mathematical concepts. Practitioners can also use resources for demonstration purposes. The resources indicated in this book will be available in most teaching situations and could be easily adapted for others. Specific resources, such as the folding star, are included as a photocopiable sheet.

Links with home

The connection between home and school is a vital one, and parents and carers need to be actively involved in ensuring the continuity of their children's education. To strengthen this link, there are specific activities and suggestions that can be tried and extended at home. Using these ideas can illustrate to parents how much fun can be gained from using mathematical activities, and this in turn will create a positive attitude towards the learning process. Where the term 'parents' is used this includes everyone who has a responsibility fot the children.

Multicultural links

Some of the activities can be used to provide multicultural links to help the children recognise that there are many different cultures and religions in the world, and that these encompass many different celebrations and festivals. Perhaps the children could count in different languages, or use counting books linked to other countries such as *Handa's Surprise* by Eileen Browne (Walker Books). The main aim is to encourage children to respect, be tolerant of, and sensitive to, the individual differences and cultural and religious backgrounds of other people.

Assessment pointers

Assessment is an everyday aspect of all teaching and learning situations and should not appear as an additional burden, but rather as a natural aspect of the learning process. Rather than adding specific assessment pointers for these activities, the Early Learning Goals have been indicated on each page to provide practitioners with a general guideline to the outcome of the task.

Numbers as labels and for counting

The ideas in this chapter focus on how children begin to use numbers as 'labels' by using mathematical language during play. The activities encourage them to count, recognise numerals and use mathematical ideas to solve practical problems.

Pass the teddy

What you need
Teddy; tape recorder; musical tape; large spotted dice; the photocopiable sheet 'Movement spinner' on page 67.

Preparation
Photocopy the movement spinner on page 67 on to card. Cut it out and insert a pencil in the centre to make it spin.

What to do
Sit the children in a circle and explain that they are going to play a game similar to 'Pass the parcel', but passing a teddy instead!

Start the music and let the children pass the teddy round the circle. When you stop the music, the child holding the teddy must stand in the centre of the circle and spin the movement spinner and roll the spotted dice, to ascertain the kind of action and the number of repeats. The child should 'read' the dice and state the number and type of movement, for example, two hops, three jumps and so on. After the child has completed the actions, they should return to their place and the game will continue.

Repeat. Ensure that each child has the opportunity to spin the spinner, roll the dice and complete the action.

Support and extension
For younger children, limit the value shown on the dice up to three dots. For older children use a dice with numbers (initially up to three), to help develop number recognition. Later a zero could be introduced on one of the faces to help the children recognise the significance of zero, for example, no jumping, no hopping and so on.

Further ideas
■ Make another spinner involving different movements, such as blinking or smiling, which could be used in a smaller group.
■ Introduce counting 'one less than' or 'one more than' the number rolled on the dice, for example, one less than three jumps, one more than two hops and so on.

LEARNING OBJECTIVES
STEPPING STONE
Use some number names accurately in play.

EARLY LEARNING GOAL
Recognise numerals 1 to 9.

GROUP SIZE
Five children.

HOME LINKS
Give the children a copy of the spinner sheet, so that they can play the game at home. Ask the children to make a list of possible movements which could be included on different movement spinners.

The magic counting wand

What you need

One metre of dowelling; insulating tape; Velcro; finger puppet; small number cards (1 to 10) with Velcro on the back.

Preparation

To make the counting wand, mark the dowelling with points at every 10cm using the insulating tape. Attach Velcro squares to these points, so that the number cards can be easily attached. Adapt the finger puppet to look like a wizard (optional). Hold the counting stick in the middle, to allow you to point to the numbers with your free hand!

What to do

Sit the children in a circle and introduce the counting wand, initially with no numbers attached. Explain to the children that this wand is going to show them a sequence of numbers.

To begin with, use only the number cards 1 to 5. Ask the children to pick up the cards, in turn, and attach them in the correct order to the counting wand. Leave the first point blank as a means of introducing zero, when appropriate.

Then, ask the children to count together, up and down the wand, as you point with finger puppet to the different numbers.

Gradually remove some of the cards – can the children still count up to 5? Ask them which numbers have been removed and how they know. Encourage explanations based on 'one more than' and 'one less than'.

Using the wand with the numbers in place, tell the children that sometimes it is a magic wand! As the children follow the finger-puppet wizard, he sometimes gets stuck or even jumps forward or backwards. The children must follow the wizard carefully and not get tricked by him. Try it!

Support and extension

With younger children, it may be necessary to use cards with dots instead of numerals. For older children, extend the sequence of numbers up to 10.

Further ideas

■ Ask the children to make up number cards to illustrate the sequence of numbers, for example, drawing one house, two houses and so on.
■ Allow a child to 'lead' the activity.

LEARNING OBJECTIVES

STEPPING STONE
Willingly attempt to count, with some numbers in the correct order.

EARLY LEARNING GOAL
Say and use number names in order in familiar contexts.

GROUP SIZE

Whole group, then repeated in smaller groups.

HOME LINKS

Ask parents to help their children look for written sequences of numbers around the home, for example, page numbers in story-books.

Counting grid

What you need
Nine sheets of A4 different coloured card; sticky tape; marker pen.

Preparation
Make a large counting grid using the nine sheets of different coloured A4 card taped together. Number the cards 1 to 9 on one side and leave the other side blank. A possible layout could be:

7	8	9
4	5	6
I	2	3

What to do
With the children seated in a large circle, introduce the counting grid. Draw attention to the blank side first and discuss the different colours seen. Ask individual children to come and stand on the blue card, pink card and so on.

Still using the blank grid, discuss the position of the different colours, using words, such as, 'below', 'above', 'under', 'beside', 'between', 'middle' and 'next to'. Invite children to come and stand on a particular card, for example, below the blue card, above the pink card and so on.

Now, turn over the grid to show the numbered side. Count aloud the numbers to the children, then repeat, asking them to count with you. Ask individual children to come and stand on a particular number, for example, 'Come and stand on number 5' or, 'Stand on a number less than 6'.

Support and extension
For younger children, arrange five or six cards in the form of a snake rather than a grid. Use pictures, along with the numerals, to help indicate number values, for example, a picture of three bears along with the number 3. Challenge older children to do simple addition, for example, stand on two numbers which will total 5 (3 and 2).

Further ideas
■ Change the layout of the grid and see if the children can still come and stand on the correct numbers.
■ Cover a numeral with a book or blank sheet of card. Can the children recognise the missing number?

LEARNING OBJECTIVES
STEPPING STONE
Use mathematical language in play.

EARLY LEARNING GOAL
Recognise numerals 1 to 9.

GROUP SIZE
Whole group, then repeated in smaller groups.

HOME LINKS
Ask parents to make a chalk grid outside or on paper and play 'Hopscotch' with their children. Encourage parents to help their children make large number symbols using stones, twigs or flowers.

9

Our counting book

What you need
Empty scrapbook or sheets of sugar paper; glue sticks; scissors; pencils and pens; magazines or gummed shapes; story-book with a very simple counting format.

What to do
Share the story-book with the children. Discuss the different features of the book, for example, the use of colour, the size (or lack) of print and how the numbers are represented. Then, tell the children that they are going to make a counting book of their own.

Show the children the empty scrapbook and ask how they think they could make their book, perhaps drawing their attention to the possible use of scissors and glue to cut out and paste in pictures.

Then, working with a small group of children look again at the story-book and any other counting books. Ask the children to experiment, by cutting and pasting or drawing their own pictures to make their own counting book. Stress the need for the pictures to be large enough to be seen, when using the book in the whole group setting. Consider how to represent the numbers, examining carefully how numerals are formed, and illustrated in different picture books.

Do not worry about a story-line or even a common thread, the important aspect is that the children have the opportunity to collect the appropriate number of items to match the chosen number. Give the children plenty of time to record the different numerals.

Allow all the children, working in small groups, to have a turn at creating a counting book. Once it is completed, use it with the whole group.

Support and extension
For younger children, consider making several counting books, perhaps one for each group of children or one book per number. Older children could start the book at zero and proceed to any appropriate number.

Further ideas
■ Make a counting book with numerals only, using different materials, for example, make 1 out of one twig, 2 out of two scraps of paper and so on.
■ Start the counting book at the biggest number and decrease down.

Lollipop number

What you need
Lolly sticks; paper plates; sticky tape; marker pen; coloured pens; scissors; glue; pictures to cut out.

Preparation
Make a set of nine lollipop number plates, by sticking a paper plate to a lolly stick. Draw or stick pictures on one side of the plate and write the corresponding numeral on the back, for example, plate 1 could have a picture of one cat, plate 2, two trees and so on.

What to do
Show the children the set of lollipop number plates and discuss the different pictures and numbers seen on them. Distribute six of the lollipop plates to individual children and ask these children to stand at the front of the group, so everyone can see their plates.

Explain that you will ask some questions and the children must hold their plate up high if they think the number on their plate is the right answer. Ask, for example, 'Who is holding plate number 3?', 'What number is one more than 2?', 'Who is holding a plate less than 5?' and questions such as, 'Who has a plate more than 2, but less than 7?'.

Ask a variety of different questions to ensure the children understand when to hold their lollipop plate up high. Give all the children in the group the opportunity to hold up the plates. The activity can be repeated in small groups.

Support and extension
For younger children, limit the value on the plates up to 5 initially and only ask direct questions, such as, 'Who is holding plate number 3?'. With older children, include the full set of plates and use more complex terms, such as, 'Hold your plate up high if your number is greater than 5 and your number is odd!'. Check on the different terms to use by referring to the 'Mathematical vocabulary booklet' (*National Numeracy Strategy*).

Further ideas
■ Roll a dice and ask the children to hold up their plate if it matches the number shown on the dice.
■ Make up two sets of the plates, so that all the children can participate.

More lollipop numbers!

What you need
Lolly sticks; paper plates; sticky tape; marker pen; coloured pens; scissors; glue; pictures to cut out.

What to do
Prepare the lollipop plates as described on page 11. Introduce the children to the lollipop plates, drawing their attention to the numerals and the corresponding pictures. Choose five children and give them the plates numbered 1 to 5 in no particular order. Ask the children to arrange themselves in a line to show the sequence of numbers from 1 to 5. Repeat the activity with different children. At a later date, introduce the full set of plates, 1 to 9, and, if appropriate, include a plate for zero (with no picture on the front and '0' on the back). Vary the sequence, starting at 9 and working down to 0, as well as starting at 0 and working upwards.

Occasionally, when distributing the plates, pretend that a plate is missing or lost and see whether the children can still arrange themselves in a line!

Support and extension
Use smaller number sequences for younger children, as appropriate to their ability. Challenge older children to a 'Guess who?' game. Ask ten children to stand at the front with their plates held up high. Tell the group you are thinking of a number and that they have to guess what it is by asking questions to which you can answer only 'yes' or 'no'. The children could ask, for example, if the number is more than 6. If your answer is 'no', the children holding up numbers 7, 8 and 9 lower their plates. The game continues until the number is correctly guessed!

Further ideas
■ Invite the children to place items on the lollipop plates to equal its number, for example, place five counters on plate number 5.
■ When all the plates have the correct number of items placed on them, ask the children to close their eyes. Remove one item and ask the children to open their eyes and spot the 'mistake'.

Move the robot!

What you need
Roamer or similar ICT model; instruction cards for moving the roamer, such as, forward→ and backward ←; number cards 1 to 10.

What to do
Show the children the roamer, drawing attention to the instruction panel on its back. Ask how they could make the roamer move forwards. Which symbol do they think should be pressed?

Teach the children to press the **forward** key followed by a **number** (to indicate the number of steps), then the **go** key. Repeat the process, showing the children how to move the roamer backwards.

Let the children experiment by moving the roamer forward and backwards a set number of steps.

Support and extension
Teach younger children only how to move the roamer forward. Challenge older children to try to predict the amount of steps required to move the roamer to a certain place, for example, how many steps it will take for the roamer to reach the door? Then ask the children to key in the number to see if they are correct.

Further ideas
■ Invite the children, in turn, to pick an instruction card (to move the roamer forwards or backwards) and a number card. They should then program the roamer to move that number of paces in the correct direction.
■ Ask a child to program the roamer to move forward three paces. Can the child press the right buttons?
■ Help the children to record the movements of the roamer by using simple sentences such as, 'I moved the roamer from the chair to the door. I pressed **forward 7** and **go**'.

LEARNING OBJECTIVES
STEPPING STONE
Instruct a programmable toy.

EARLY LEARNING GOAL
Use developing mathematical ideas and methods to solve practical problems.

GROUP SIZE
Whole group, then one or two children at a time.

HOME LINKS
Enquire if parents have any programmable toys (aircraft, toy cars) that they could bring in to show the children. Ask parents to take their children to visit a toy shop to see the range of toys that move.

Brilliant bugs

What you need
The photocopiable sheet 'Bug cards' on page 68; a dice with spots to indicate 1, 1, 2, 2, 3, 3.

Preparation
Copy on to card the photocopiable sheet on page 68 to create a set of the bug cards. Ensure there are sufficient bug cards for your group size.

What to do
Show the children the bug cards and draw their attention to the number of bugs on each card. Ask the children to roll the dice, count the spots out loud and to select the matching bug card, for example, if the dice shows two spots, the card with two bugs should be picked up.

Continue playing until all the bug cards have been picked up – each child should end up with three or four cards. During the game, ask questions such as, 'Which number have you thrown on the dice?', 'Which bug card will you pick up?' and so on.

The winner is the player who has the highest total of bugs when all their cards are added together. Alternatively, just play for fun.

Support and extension
Simplify the game for younger children by using cards with only one or two bugs. For older children, place all the cards face down, so they can not see the number of bugs and, once they have rolled the dice, they should pick up the corresponding number of cards (rather than the number of bugs). When all the cards have been collected, they can be turned over and the total number of bugs counted.

Further idea
■ Use the bug cards to play a pelmanism or memory-type game with pairs of children. Place the bug cards face down on the table and ask the children, one at a time, to turn over two cards. If they match, the child keeps the pair, if not, they are returned. The winner is the player with most pairs when all the cards have been picked up.

Number tiddlywinks

What you need
The photocopiable sheet 'Number squares' on page 69; counters to use as tiddlywinks; scissors.

Preparation
Make a copy of the photocopiable sheet on page 69 for each child.

What to do
Give a copy of the number square sheet to each child. Discuss the numbers with the children, asking them to point to specific numbers on the sheet, for example, a number more than 3, a number one less than 5 and so on.

Help the children to cut up the sheet along the dotted lines into six squares. Then, ask the children to pick up, for instance, card number 4, card number 3 and so on. Invite the children to place the cards, in order, from number 1 to 6 or from number 6 down to 1.

Place the cards face up on the table. Use the counters as in the game of 'Tiddlywinks', challenging the children to flick a counter on to card number 1. Count with the children how many attempts it takes to succeed. Then, continue the game with the next number, and so on. Discuss how far, or how near, the cards should be to one another, and what might make the game easier.

The winner is the player who gets their counters on to all six cards first. Alternatively, play on until each child is a winner!

Support and extension
Use just four cards with younger children. At the beginning of the game, to help reinforce the number values, ask each child to place the correct number of counters on each number card. For older children, add more number squares for the children to continue the game.

Further ideas
■ Place the cards face up and ask the children to pick up cards which total a specified number, such as, two cards which add up to ten (the 6 and 4 card), adapting the game to the needs of the children.
■ Shuffle cards, 1 to 3, with the bug cards on the photocopiable sheet on page 68 and play a game of 'Snap!'.

Bags of numbers!

What you need
Plastic self-seal bags (A4 size); small items to place in the bags (such as, counters, toys, shells, construction blocks); pieces of card; tape; washing line and pegs. Note: Never leave young children unattended when using plastic bags.

What to do
Working with the children in small groups, make a set of 1 to 5 number bags, by placing a different number of items in large self-seal plastic bags. Allow the children to choose which items should go in each bag, encouraging them to consider different 'mixes', for example, four construction blocks together, or one shell, one construction block and two elephant counters together.

Ask the children to count the number of items in each bag and to say the amount out loud. Use pieces of card to indicate the correct number, for example, write the number 5 one side of the card and draw five dots on the other. To stop little fingers opening the bags, it is a good idea to seal them with tape!

Gather all the children together and show them the washing line. Ask the children to peg the number bags, in number sequence, from 1 to 5 or from 5 to 1. Later re-distribute the bags in a random order and ask the children to re-order them on the washing line.

Support and extension
For younger children, limit the number of bags to three. For older children, make a set of 11 bags with numbers 0 to 10, and discuss with the children why the zero bag is empty.

Further ideas
■ Ask the children to close their eyes, while you remove a bag or exchange two bags. Challenge the children to spot the 'mistake'.

■ Using the number bags pegged on the washing line, ask a child to fetch a bag in answer to different questions posed, for example, 'Can you find a bag which is one more than 3?' or, 'Can you find a bag with an even number?'.

Hide-and-seek the number!

What you need
Set of number bags (see the activity 'Bags of numbers!' on page 16), washing line. Note: never leave young children unattended when using plastic bags.

What to do
Show the children the number bags, reminding them of the various items included in each bag and how the number card indicates the amount inside.

Select one of the bags and count aloud the number of items in it. Place the bag behind your back and grasp a corner of it along with some of the items. Now show the bag once more to the children, still holding the corner, and ask them to guess how many items are hidden in your hand.

If you choose bag number 4, for example, and the children can see three items remaining in the bag, they need to work out that you have one item hidden in your hand. Demonstrate to the children how they can hold up four fingers, then fold down three to indicate the number of remaining items, to show the correct answer.

Once the children have guessed correctly, show them the hidden item. Repeat the activity using different bags and hiding different amounts.

Support and extension
Adapt this game to the needs and requirements of the children within your group. With younger children limit the numbers used. Challenge older children to solve more complex number problems.

Further ideas
■ Invite a child to do the 'hiding'. Use the bags flat on the table and provide a cup or cloth to cover up some of the items.
■ Ask the children to record the work by drawing the bag and its items.

LEARNING OBJECTIVES
STEPPING STONE
Count an irregular arrangement of up to 10 objects.

EARLY LEARNING GOAL
Use developing mathematical ideas and methods to solve practical problems.

GROUP SIZE
Whole group and small group.

HOME LINKS
Encourage the children to ask their parents if they have seen a magician who 'hides' items which then reappear!

Roll the dice!

LEARNING OBJECTIVES

STEPPING STONE
Count out up to 6 objects from a larger group.

EARLY LEARNING GOAL
Count reliably up to 10 everyday objects.

GROUP SIZE
Any size.

What you need
Assortment of different dices (such as spotty, number, colour and shape dice); items to be counted, such as counters or similar; number square cards 1 to 6 for each child from the photocopiable sheet on page 69 (see the activity, 'Number tiddlywinks' on page 15).

Preparation
A large dice is a useful item in any setting, and it can easily be made from an old tissue box. Most supermarkets and chemists sell tissues in cube-shaped boxes or hexagonal prism-shaped boxes. By strengthening the faces, these can easily be converted into dice. The six faces can be decorated and used as a colour dice, a spotty dice, a number dice or a shape dice.

What to do
Sit together in a circle. Roll the spotty dice and ask an individual, or the whole group, to hold up that many fingers, to fetch that many items, to count aloud that many counters into a container, to jump up that many times, to shout out their name that many times, and so on. Repeat the activity using the different dice and suggesting different challenges for the children to complete.

In a small group, distribute the number square cards and ask the children to arrange them in a line from 1 to 6. Explain that they are going to roll the dice and if, for example, they roll a three, they can turn over card number 3, and so on. The winner is the first to turn all their cards over!

Support and extension
Use fewer number cards with younger children and play until all the cards are turned over, rather than declaring a winner. With older children play the number square game with the rule that the numbers have to be rolled in sequence starting at 1 or 6.

Further ideas
■ Use a large colour dice for a matching game. Ask the child to roll the dice and then to find an item in the same colour on the table.
■ Repeat the above game using a shape dice, where the child matches the shape on the dice to a similar shaped item.

Numbers as sets

This chapter provides ideas on how to use numbers as 'sets', focusing on adding and taking away objects from a group. Children will be encouraged to use vocabulary involved in addition and subtraction with confidence and to offer solutions to number problems.

How many teddies?

What you need
The photocopiable sheet 'Teddy grid' on page 70; coloured felt-tipped pens.

Preparation
Prepare the photocopiable sheet by colouring the teddies and folding along the lines. This enables the grid to be folded in different ways to 'show' and to 'hide' different teddies. You may find it helpful to have a large copy (A3 size) for yourself and smaller versions (A4 size) for the children.

What to do
Introduce the teddy grid by counting the number of bears on the page. Repeat this several times, counting the teddies from different starting points.

Ensure that the children realise that the number of teddies remains the same regardless of the order in which they are counted. Fold the grid, so that only two teddies are showing. Discuss how the grid was folded.

Offer a child the grid and ask them to fold it to also show two teddies. Did the child fold the grid in the same way, or differently?

Continue asking the children in the group to fold and show other numbers of bears. If appropriate, introduce different terms to them, such as 'more than' and 'less than'.

Support and extension
With younger children, use a grid with fewer teddies. It may also be helpful to colour the teddies in six different colours to make comparison easier for the children.

Introduce older children to simple subtraction by folding the grid to show two teddies, then ask how many teddies are hiding. Remind the children that there were six teddies to begin with. Suggest the children hold up six fingers, then fold down two fingers (to represent the seen teddies). How many of the fingers are still standing?

Further ideas
■ Cut up a copy of the teddy grid and use the bears to make different-sized sets of teddies. Discuss with the children which set has the most, or the least, teddy bears.
■ Make a larger grid with ten teddies.

Top that tower!

What you need
Interlocking blocks (such as, LEGO or DUPLO); dice marked +1, +1, +1, –1, –1, –1.

What to do
Invite the children to each count out five blocks and build a tower with them. Then, ask each child, in turn, to roll the dice. If the dice shows +1, a block is added to the tower. If the dice shows –1, a block is removed.

The player with the tallest tower after five rounds is the winner. Throughout the game, ask questions such as, 'Who has the most blocks?', 'Who has the shortest tower?', 'If you add one more block, how many blocks will you have in your tower?'

If you find it appropriate, modify the dice to have four +1 faces and two –1 faces, or try other combinations in the game, such as using two dice, or missing a go if you roll a particular number. Discuss the relevance of the different outcomes, drawing the children's attention to the best, and worst, outcome as the dice is rolled.

Support and extension
For younger children, use a dice with just three spots and play the game using addition only. With older children consider varying the game, so that the winner is the player with shortest tower!

Further ideas
■ Start the game with each child having a tower of five blocks and using a dice with one to three spots. This time if the player rolls a two, for example, two blocks are removed from their tower and are given to the child on the left. This player adds these blocks to their tower. The game continues in this way – the children discarding blocks to their left, but receiving blocks from their right. The winner is the first to discard all their blocks! This activity works best in a group of five or six children.
■ The above game can be varied, so that the player who first makes a ten-block tower wins the game.

Dice games galore

What you need
Assortment of dice, such as spotty dice and numeral dice; coloured counters or other small items such as toy bricks or small-world people; paper plates.

Preparation
Make some large dice out of tissue boxes – see the activity 'Roll the dice!' on page 18 for more details.

What to do
Invite the children to sit in a large circle and introduce the dice with one to three spots. Choose two children to begin the game.

Ask the first child to roll the dice and count out that number of items, such as counters, on to a paper plate. The second child then rolls the dice and counts out their score on to another paper plate.

Then ask the children to compare the number of items on both plates and to say who has the most. Encourage the children to speak in simple sentences, such as: 'I have three counters. Billy has two counters. I have more counters than Billy'.

Repeat the activity with other pairs of children. If two children roll the same number on the dice, try and encourage them to say for example, 'I have one counter and Anna also has one counter. We both have the same'.

Support and extension
With younger children, be ready to offer support as necessary with both counting the items and when comparing the amounts. Encourage older children to use the term 'less than' in their comparisons, for example, 'I have two counters, Mark has three counters. I have less counters than Mark'.

Further ideas
■ Use a variety of different dice, if applicable, and extend the activity to a fuller range of numbers.
■ In a circle, ask each child to roll the dice and to jump/clap one more than (or one less than) the number displayed on the dice. Ask the rest of the children in the circle to help by counting out loud the number of jumps or claps.

Dice game discovery

What you need
Dice with one to six spots; cloth bag; items for counting purposes (such as counters, plastic bears and so on).

What to do
Sit together in a large group. Choose a child to secretly roll the dice and then to count that number of items into a cloth bag.

Invite the other children to work out which number was rolled on the dice, by counting the number of items in the cloth bag. Repeat the activity several times with different children rolling the dice.

Once the children are comfortable with the game, ask a child to roll the dice in secret, but, this time, to count into the bag one more item than the number shown on the dice. Challenge the children to work out which number was rolled on the dice. Then, repeat the activity, this time suggesting the child places one less item into the cloth bag.

Support and extension
Different types of dice can be used depending on the age and ability of the children within the group. With younger children use a dice with three spots. Challenge older children, if appropriate, to use a dice with numbers 1-6 or even a spinner with numbers 1-10.

Further ideas
■ Roll two dice with one to three spots without the children seeing the numbers thrown. Tell the children the total score and ask them to guess the two numbers rolled on the dice.

■ Ask the children to match the number rolled on a dice to a number card. Then, after a few number cards have been collected, invite the children to arrange these cards in either ascending and descending order.

■ Play a game with the children where you roll the dice and let the children see the top number. They then have to work out what the number on the bottom of the dice will be without looking. (The total of opposite faces on a dice is always seven, therefore, if one is on the top face, six will be hidden at the bottom.) Help the children to work out the answer by holding up seven fingers and then folding down the amount of fingers shown on the dice. How many fingers are still standing?

1	2	3	4	5	6
IIII I	I	III	I	II	I

Lacing beads

What you need
Different coloured beads; thread or lace for each child; set of number square cards on the photocopiable sheet on page 69.

Preparation
Make a set of number square cards on the photocopiable sheet on page 69. (See also the activity 'Number tiddlywinks' on page 15.)

What to do
Place the number square cards face down in the centre of the table and give each child a thread or lace. Ask one child to select a card and to say the number out loud. All the children in the group must then pick up that same number of beads (each child choosing one colour for that quantity) and thread them onto their lace.

Another child should then pick a card and say the number and all the children should thread that number of beads on to their lace. (This amount of beads should again be the same colour, but can be a different colour to previous set.)

Continue until the laces are full of beads. Throughout the activity, ask the children questions, such as, 'How many beads are on your lace?', 'Have you all got the same amount of beads?' and, 'Can you remember how many times we picked up card number 2?'.

Support and extension
With younger children, initially use only number square cards 1 to 3. With older children, let each child turn over an individual card and put that number of beads on to their lace, so that the amounts of threaded beads vary. Ask the children to compare their laces.

Further ideas
■ Ask a child to secretly turn over a card and thread that number of beads on to their lace. Can the other children identify the number on the card?
■ Invite the children to thread ten beads on to their lace. Then each child, in turn, should take a number card and remove that amount of beads from their thread. The winner is the first to remove all their beads.

LEARNING OBJECTIVES
STEPPING STONE
Count out up to six objects from a larger group.

EARLY LEARNING GOAL
Recognise numerals 1 to 9.

GROUP SIZE
Small group.

HOME LINKS
Suggest that parents help their children play threading games at home, perhaps using cotton reels and shoe laces. Ask if any of the children have a bead kit at home and if they have made any colourful necklaces and bracelets, suggest they bring them in to show the other children.

Number-bead laces

What you need
Six laces; 21 beads; set of number square cards on the photocopiable sheet on page 69.

Preparation
Make up a set of one to six number-bead laces, by threading one bead on one lace, two on the next, and so on, up to six. Use different colours and patterns of beads on the laces as you wish. You can also thread the beads so that the children are able to slide them up and down the lace, but this is not essential. As the beads are threaded on to the lace, they are never lost and this is always an advantage when working with young children!

What to do
Take a four-bead lace and count aloud the number of beads with the children. Ask the children to select laces with less (or more) beads, a lace with one more than (one less than) four, and so on. Repeat the activity using the different number-bead laces.

Now, select two different number-bead laces and ask the children to compare them. Help the children by asking which is the longest (and the shortest) length. Show the children how to find the difference between the laces by matching them up and identifying the 'extra' beads.

Using a five-bead lace, demonstrate how the beads can be separated to illustrate the numerous ways of making a total of five (for example, three beads, gap, two beads; four beads, gap, one bead). Continue in this way with different number-bead laces.

Support and extension
For younger children, limit the number-bead laces to four and ensure that each activity is fully understood before proceeding to the next. If appropriate practise simple addition and subtraction with older children.

Further ideas
■ Using the number square cards, pick up a card and ask a child to find the corresponding number-bead lace.
■ Extend the above activity, by asking a child to find a number-bead lace which is one more than or one less than the number on the card.

How many beads?

What you need
A set of number-bead laces (see activity 'Number-bead laces' on page 24).

What to do
Take a six-bead lace and count aloud with the children the number of beads. Position the lace behind your back and hide some of the beads by concealing them in your fist. Now re-show the bead lace to the children asking: 'Can you remember how many beads were on the lace?', 'How many beads can you now see?', 'How many beads are hidden in my fist?'.

Encourage the children to think of different ways to work out the answer, such as writing marks on paper, using fingers and so on.

Give the children different number-bead laces and ask them to count how many beads they have on their lace. Say to the group, for example: 'Hold your lace up if the number of beads on your lace is less than five', 'Hold your lace up if the number of beads on your lace is more than two' and so on. Re-distribute the number-bead laces within the group so that you can repeat the activity.

Support and extension
Modify the questions asked to individual children to match their understanding and knowledge. Limit the number-bead laces to four for younger children. For older children, increase the number-bead laces to 10.

Further ideas
■ Using different bead lengths for each child, slide the beads, one at a time, to illustrate number bonds, for example, using the six-bead lace, slide the beads to show five and one; four and two; three and three.
■ Ask the children to try to record the number bonds on paper with drawings and numerals, if appropriate.

LEARNING OBJECTIVES
STEPPING STONE
Sometimes show confidence and offer solutions to problems.

EARLY LEARNING GOAL
Begin to relate addition to combining two groups of objects and subtraction to 'taking away'.

GROUP SIZE
Small group.

HOME LINKS
Ask parents to help make number bonds at home by placing sets of fruit, sweets or biscuits on to one plate and then transferring them, one at a time, to another plate. Suggest that the children might like to record their 'experiments' on paper and bring them in to show the other children.

Bingo!

LEARNING OBJECTIVES
STEPPING STONE
Recognise numerals 1 to 5, then 1 to 9.

EARLY LEARNING GOAL
Recognise numerals 1 to 9.

GROUP SIZE
Small group.

What you need
Dice with one to six spots; counters; the photocopiable sheet 'Bingo boards' on page 71.

Preparation
Copy the photocopiable sheet on page 71 so that there are enough for one gameboard per child. Cut out the boards.

What to do
Give each child a gameboard and some counters. Ask the children to point to the numerals on the gameboard as you count from one to six to ensure they recognise all the numbers.

Explain that they are going to play a game of 'Bingo' by rolling the dice and then covering the number scored with a counter.

Invite the first player to roll the dice and to put a counter on the matching number on the gameboard. Continue with each child taking a turn to roll the dice and placing the counters on the correct numbers.

If a number is rolled on the dice which is already covered with a counter on the gameboard, the player misses a go. The winner is the first to have counters on all six numbers.

This game can also be played in reverse. The numbers are initially covered and counters are removed as the dice is rolled. The winner is the first to remove all their counters!

Support and extension
For younger children, limit the numbers on the gameboard to 1 to 4. If appropriate, use a spotty dice and modify the gameboard to have spots instead of numerals.

Challenge older children to use a gameboard with eight numbers, from 2 to 9. In this version, the players use two dice, one numbered from 1 to 6 and the other, 1 to 3. The child rolls both dice and adds the score together, before placing the counter on the correct number.

Further ideas
■ Extend the 'Addition bingo' described above to incorporate subtraction. The dice numbered 1 to 6 is rolled first, followed by the dice numbered 1 to 3. The second number is subtracted from the first and the counter is placed accordingly.
■ Modify the gameboards by omitting some numbers and repeating others.

HOME LINKS
Ask the children if they know anyone in their family who goes to play 'Bingo'. Encourage the children to play 'Bingo' at home with their family. (Many retailers sell bingo-type games.)

Extraordinary egg-boxes

What you need
Egg box for each child; dice with one to three spots; counters; sticky dots; marker pen; colouring materials or paints (optional)

Preparation
Mark each 'hole' in each egg-box with dots or numerals up to the value of three.

What to do
Give each child an egg-box. Invite each child in turn to roll the dice and place the corresponding amount of counters in their egg-box. For instance, if the dice shows two, the player places two counters in the correctly numbered 'hole' in their egg-box.

The winner is the first person to fill their six holes with the correct number of counters.

Ask the children questions as the game is played, for example, 'What have you rolled on your dice?', 'How many counters do you need to pick up?', 'Where will you place those counters?' and so on.

Support and extension
Simplify the activity for younger children by using only half the egg-box. For older children, the game can be extended to use numbers up to six.

Further ideas
■ Ask the children to decorate their egg-box using colouring materials or paints to make them more fun to use.
■ Play the game in reverse, so that the children start with their egg-boxes full of counters and take them out depending on numbers rolled on the dice. The winner is the first to empty their egg-box.
■ The egg-boxes used to play the game do not have to be identical, as different numbers could be repeated.
■ Vary the type of dice used, including zero on one face and addition or subtraction sums on other faces, for example, 3 + 1 or 2 – 1.

LEARNING OBJECTIVES
STEPPING STONE
Show an interest in numbers and counting.

EARLY LEARNING GOAL
Say and use number names in order in familiar contexts.

GROUP SIZE
Small group.

HOME LINKS
Ask the children to collect different types of egg-boxes. Suggest that parents help their children collect different small items to fill an egg-box numbered 1–6, for example, one button, two paper clips and so on.

Bears on a plate

What you need
A set of Compare Bears, Three Bear family, Linking Elephants or similar; set of ten paper plates with the numerals 0 to 9 (one number per plate).

What to do
Give a paper plate to each child and ask them to place the correct number of bears on each plate to match the numeral indicated on it, for example, five bears on plate 5. Repeat the activity several times gradually using the full set of plates. Care should be taken when introducing the zero plate to ensure the children understand that nothing should be placed on this plate.

   Play the game again, placing bears on all the plates, but this time make several 'mistakes'. Challenge the children to spot the mistakes!

Support and extension
For younger children, use plates with the numberals 1 to 6 initially. For older children, introduce number cards, or roll a dice, to indicate how many bears should be placed on the plates.

LEARNING OBJECTIVES
STEPPING STONE
Say with confidence the number that is one more than a given number.

EARLY LEARNING GOAL
Use language such as 'more' or 'less' to compare two numbers.

GROUP SIZE
Small group.

Further ideas
■ Give each child an empty, blank plate. Ask them to place three bears on their plate. Then, invite them to place one more bear on the plate. How many bears are there now?
■ Extend the above activity to include subtraction, by reducing the number of bears on the plate.
■ Distribute all the numbered plates and ask the children to position them in order starting from zero.
■ Give out a reduced set of plates (such as 2, 5, 1, 8 and 4). Challenge the children to place these plates in numerical order.

HOME LINKS
Ask parents to let their children help count out biscuits on to a plate, so that each family member has a biscuit. Suggest that parents provide paper plates and simple food items (biscuits and so on) for their children to share out among their toys for a pretend party.

Heads I win, tails you lose!

What you need
The photocopiable sheet 'Heads or tails?' on page 72; two different coloured counters; coin; dice.

Preparation
Photocopy the sheet on page 72, so that there will be one gameboard per pair of children.

What to do
Introduce the gameboard to the children, commenting on the use of pictures and the lack of numbers. Invite the children to play a game, not with a dice, but with a coin!

Show how the coin can be tossed and explain that if it lands on 'heads', the player moves forward one square, but if it lands on 'tails', the player moves back one square.

Give the children a counter each and ask them to position their counters at the beginning of the road.

Each child in turn tosses the coin and moves their counter either forwards or backwards accordingly. (If the player cannot go backwards, they miss that go.) The winner is the player to reach the end of the road first.

Support and extension
For younger children, it may be helpful to use a dice with one to three spots. Extend the game for older children by introducing a dice marked +1, +1, +1, –1, –1, –1, once they are familiar with using the coin.

Further ideas
■ Write the numerals, 1 to 11, on the gameboard. In this version of the game, one player starts on 1, the other 11. Use a coin or a dice marked +1 and –1.
■ Start the game, by placing counters at the mid-point of the road.

How many ways?

What you need
Three hoops or grouping circles or pieces of rope.

What to do
Invite the children to sit in a large circle. Explain that you have a problem – you cannot decide how many different ways to arrange three different items. Ask the children to help you solve the problem.

Position three hoops, grouping circles or rope to form three different sets in the centre of the room and select three children to assist you.

First, ask all three children to stand together in one hoop, then ask two to remain in that hoop, while one moves to another, finally ask each child to stand alone in each hoop. Progress slowly through this activity, asking for suggestions from the children on where their friends should stand, so that the initial problem can be solved.

Repeat the activity, this time finding out how many different ways four items can be arranged.

LEARNING OBJECTIVES
STEPPING STONE
Separate a group of three or four objects in different ways, beginning to recognise that the total is still the same.

EARLY LEARNING GOAL
In practical activities and discussion begin to use the vocabulary involved in adding and subtracting.

GROUP SIZE
Whole group.

Support and extension
For younger children, work with pairs of children and encourage them to sort small table-top items in different ways. Show older children how to record the above activity on paper using mathematical terms, for example, $1 + 1 + 1 = 3$, $2 + 1 = 3$ and $3 + 0 = 3$.

Further ideas
■ Take photographs of the children standing in the different sets of hoops.
■ Make a wall display to illustrate the activity. Use a combination of the children's drawings and recordings as well as the photographs you have taken and written explanations.

HOME LINKS
Ask parents to help their children find out how many different four fruit combinations could be arranged in a bowl, for example, 4 apples, 3 apples and 1 banana, and so on.

Rhymes and stories

Ideas in this chapter encourage children to use mathematical language in play, through taking part in songs, stories and games, this will help them to count reliably up to ten and use number names in familiar contexts. Some activities will encourage children to show confidence and offer solutions to problems.

Mrs Wishy-Washy washes

What you need
Low-level washing line; variety of socks in different sizes and colours; the photocopiable sheet 'Mrs Wishy-Washy' on page 73.

Preparation
Enlarge the photocopiable rhyme 'Mrs Wishy-Washy' to A3 size, so that it can be displayed when singing with the children.

What to do
Show the children the socks and explain that Mrs Wishy-Washy has been washing and needs to hang out her socks to dry on the washing line.

Ask individual children to hang socks on the line while you and the children sing and repeat the first two verses of the rhyme, 'Mrs Wishy-Washy', to the tune of 'Here We Go Round the Mulberry Bush'. Ask a child to count the socks on the line and, so, answer the rhyme.

Rearrange the number, colour, size and length of the socks on the line and ask different questions by singing the other verses of the rhyme.

Support and extension
For younger children, repeat the game in small groups, so that all of them are given the opportunity to peg up and count the socks on the line. Also, it may be appropriate to limit the number of socks they can use. Encourage older children to differentiate between different coloured socks, short/long socks, patterned or plain socks, and then challenge them to link up two attributes such as short patterned socks!

■■

Further ideas
■ If preferred, you could make cardboard socks rather than use real ones. (This could be used as an activity for the children.)
■ Introduce the notion of pairs of socks, and ask how many pairs of socks are on the line.
■ Arrange the socks in a pattern on the line (for example, red, blue, red, blue) and challenge the children to continue the pattern.

LEARNING OBJECTIVES
STEPPING STONE
Enjoy joining in with number rhymes and songs.

EARLY LEARNING GOAL
Count reliably up to 10 everyday objects.

GROUP SIZE
Large group, then repeated in smaller groups.

HOME LINKS
Ask parents to let their children help sort the socks at home. Suggest that the children try to make a list (either in words or pictorially) of the different types of socks they can find, for example, short socks for the summer, sports socks, cartoon socks, musical socks and so on.

Square dancing

What you need
Large, open space; the photocopiable sheet 'Square dancing' on page 74.

Preparation
Enlarge the photocopiable sheet on page 74 to an A3 size.

What to do
Using the photocopiable sheet as a guide, teach the children the square-dance routine starting with pairs of children and extending to the whole group if space allows. Say the words at quite a lively pace, adding a few 'yippees' along the way!

The wording can easily be modified as required. It can be shortened to:

Forward three steps, Turn to your right. (x 4)
Now we're ready to start again!

Alternatively, you can make changes such as, 'Turn to your left' (rather than turning to the right) or, 'Step back' (rather than stepping forward). Also, instead of clapping, the children could nod their heads and, rather than stamping their feet, they could jump or hop forward and back.

Draw the children's attention to the shape of the dance – it forms four sides of a square. Ask if the children could think of ways to change it to be a rectangle (by varying the number of steps), or even to another shape – try triangles and diamonds.

Support and extension
For younger children, use the shortened version of the dance and gradually extend it as appropriate. Encourage older children to extend the dance, making up new sequences of actions.

Further ideas
■ Take a walk around your setting and then describe it, for example, 'We walked along the path quickly, then turned right slowly into the corridor. We passed a door on the left and a window on the right...'.
■ Make up a clapping or stamping sequence linked to counting, for example, stamp your feet on every even number and clap your hands on five and ten.

LEARNING OBJECTIVES
STEPPING STONE
Observe and use positional language.

EARLY LEARNING GOAL
Talk about, recognise and re-create simple patterns.

GROUP SIZE
Whole group and/or small groups.

HOME LINKS
Encourage the parents to take their children on a short walk and then describe it together, based on the number of steps, turns, directions and so on. Suggest that parents play a game with their children, where the child is a robot and the parent gives them instructions (forward three steps, turn to the right). Reverse roles, so the parent becomes the robot and the child gives the instructions.

How many in our book?

What you need
The counting book from the activity 'Our counting book' on page 10.

Preparation
You will need to have already completed the activity 'Our counting book' on page 10 with the children.

What to do
Show the children the counting book which they made previously, reminding them how and when they made it. Read the book through with the children, drawing attention to their pictures and the numerals depicted. Invite the children to help with the counting, perhaps counting the characters from the picture pages or counting the patterns formed.

As you read, take time to stop and ask the children to suggest which number will be come next. Ask them how certain they are, for example, that four will follow three.

Encourage different children to pick out and describe the picture they made for the book and to say which number the picture represents. If several counting books were created, comparison could be made between different pages of the same number. Display the counting book, so that it is accessible for the children to look at again.

Support and extension
For younger children, concentrate on the numerals 1 to 5. For older children use the book to show the numbers in both ascending and descending order. Challenge the children to 'retell' the story from memory.

Further ideas
■ Tell traditional stories, such as 'Goldilocks and the Three Bears', 'The Three Little Pigs' and so on, and encourage the children to count the characters (and chairs, beds, houses and so on) and act out the story.
■ Encourage the children to produce artwork (paintings, drawings or collages) based on these traditional stories and create a wall display, showing numbers as well as pictures.

Old MacDonald had a farm

LEARNING OBJECTIVES
STEPPING STONE
Enjoy joining in with number rhymes and songs.

EARLY LEARNING GOAL
Say and use number names in order in familiar contexts.

GROUP SIZE
Whole group.

What you need
Copy of the traditional rhyme 'Old MacDonald Had a Farm'; props, such as finger puppets, soft toys or face masks, to represent the different animals.

What to do
Seat the children on the carpet and ask if any of them have visited a farm. Tell the children that you recently visited a farm and that the old farmer was called Mr MacDonald. He had a large farm with lots of different animals.

Ask for suggestions regarding possible animals that could live on Mr MacDonald's farm (cows, sheep, horses, goats, hens, ducks, geese, cats, dogs).

Explain that it was a rather noisy farm, as all the different animals were making a dreadful noise. Ask the children what sort of noise the cow might make. Gradually go through the noises of most of the animals mentioned.

Now introduce the animal props and ask some of the children to represent the different animals, by wearing a mask or holding a puppet or toy.

Sing the rhyme 'Old MacDonald Had a Farm', using the children's suggestions and increasing the number of the animals per verse:

Old MacDonald had a farm,
E – I – E – I – O.
And on that farm he had one cow,
E – I – E – I – O.
With a moo-moo here,
And a moo-moo there,
Here a moo,
There a moo,
Everywhere a moo-moo.
Old MacDonald had a farm,
E – I – E – I – O.

For the following verses include, for example, two ducks quacking, three dogs barking, four sheep bleating and so on.

Support and extension
For younger children have only one of each type of animal, or increase the number of animals, but keep to the same species. Ask older children questions regarding the rhyme such as, how many cows were mooing? Which animal followed the dogs? How many animals were there altogether?

HOME LINKS
Suggest that parents take their children to visit a local farm. Alternatively, organise a group outing with parent helpers. Find out if any of the parents are able to bring in a farm animal, such as chicks, lambs or sheepdogs, to show the children.

Further ideas
■ Link the animals included to other themes, for example, animals in a zoo, animals at the seaside, animals in the jungle, and so on.
■ Start with five animals and work down to one. Can the children remember which number comes next?

One and two and three...

What you need
Large numeral cards 1 to 8.

Preparation
Familiarise yourself with the rhyme below, which is sung to the tune 'Heads and Shoulders, Knees and Toes'. The rhyme is very easy to remember and can easily be modified as necessary.

What to do
Sing the following song through slowly to the children and point to the relevant numeral card as you sing:

> *One and two and three and four,*
> *Three and four.*
> *One and two and three and four,*
> *Three and four.*
> *And five and six and seven and eight.*
> *One and two and three and four,*
> *Three and four.*

When the children are familiar with the rhyme, ask eight volunteers to stand at the front to hold the numeral cards. Ask the children to hold their card up high as the number is sung! Sing the rhyme quite slowly at first, picking up pace as you go.

Alter the rhyme by omitting a number, for example, 'One and... and three and four'. Can the children remember to omit 'two' throughout the rhyme!

Vary your tone and volume when singing the rhyme, or whisper the odd numbers and shout the even numbers!

Support and extension
The rhyme could be modified for younger children to include only the numbers one to four. For older children, consider starting the rhyme at 'eight' and descending in order back down to one.

Further ideas
■ Rather than singing the rhyme in numerical order, consider following the order of cards as the children hold them to assist in number recognition. Ask the children with the 1 to 8 number cards to stand in a random number order and everyone then sings the rhyme accordingly.
■ Use other number rhymes with the children, such as, 'Five Little Speckled Frogs', 'One Potato, Two Potato' and 'Five Currant Buns' (all Traditional).

Five brown teddies

What you need
Five toy teddies; the photocopiable sheet 'Teddies on the wall' on page 75.

Preparation
Familiarise yourself with the song 'Five brown teddies' below, which is sung to the tune 'Ten Green Bottles' (Traditional). Ensure there are sufficient copies of the photocopiable sheet, one for each child. Prepare the sheets by cutting between the teddies, so that the bears can be folded down. Place the toy teddies on a table (representing a wall).

What to do
Teach the children the song:

Five brown teddies sitting on a wall,
Five brown teddies sitting on a wall,
And if one brown teddy should accidentally fall,
There'd be four brown teddies sitting on the wall.

Sing the song together, removing the teddies from the table, one at a time. Ask the children questions such as, 'How many teddies are sitting on the wall?' or, 'How many teddies have fallen?'.

Give each child a copy of the photocopiable sheet and discuss the pictures. Count aloud together how many teddies are on the wall. Show how the children can fold down a teddy, to illustrate a teddy 'falling' from the wall.

Sing the song as a whole group with the children demonstrating, by folding, how the teddies 'fall' from the wall. Stop at different verses of the song, asking individual children to show how many teddies are on the wall and how many have fallen.

Support and extension
Act out the song using the toy teddies only with younger children, progressing to paper teddies when they are older. If appropriate, limit the number of teddies to three. For older children, the number of teddies sitting on the wall could be extended to nine or ten.

Further ideas
■ Introduce simple subtraction with the teddies. Let two teddies fall from the wall and ask how many teddies have fallen.
■ Hold a teddy bears' picnic in the setting.

Down to zero!

What you need
A counting-down story-book, such as *Rocket Countdown* by Nick Sharratt (Walker Books). Other possible books include *Ten Little Babies* by Lisa Kopper (Frances Lincoln Ltd), *Ten, Nine, Eight* by Molly Bang (Red Fox) or rhymes, such as 'Ten in the Bed' or 'Ten Green Bottles'.

What to do
Read the story or rhyme to the children, encouraging the children to comment and discuss it. Prompt the children with questions, such as, 'Who noticed the use of numbers in this story (rhyme)?', 'Can anybody remember any of the numbers?', 'Which order were the numbers in – did they go up or down?', 'What was the first number?' and, 'What was the last number?'.

Repeat the story or rhyme several times, encouraging all the children to participate by counting in unison slowly and clearly down to zero. Suggest that the children try holding up ten fingers, gradually folding down one at a time to reach zero. (Co-ordinating fingers with counting is difficult and takes time to learn!)

Alternatively, invite them to shout out 'ZERO' or 'BLAST OFF!' at the end of the story/ rhyme and encourage the children to jump up high in the air.

Support and extension
For younger children, adapt the book or rhyme to start at five rather than ten and build up gradually. Invite older children to hold up numeral cards from ten to zero, to form a simple number line.

Further ideas
■ Using the story or counting rhyme, encourage the children to act out the sequences.
■ Invite the children to make simple rockets (from DUPLO, cardboard boxes and so on) to use with the countdown.

LEARNING OBJECTIVES
STEPPING STONE
Show curiosity about numbers by offering comments or asking questions.

EARLY LEARNING GOAL
Say and use number names in order in familiar contexts.

GROUP SIZE
Large group and/or small groups.

HOME LINKS
Tell parents that the children are learning to count down to zero and ask if they can help their child to practise at home. Ask parents to read stories to their children which follow a counting-down sequence of numbers.

Clap and sing - all day long!

What you need
Familiarise yourself with the song 'All Day Long', which is sung to the tune of 'The Wheels on the Bus' (Traditional).

What to do
Stand in a circle together and sing the song:

> My hands can clap both high and low,
> High and low, high and low,
> My hands can clap both high and low,
> All day long.
>
> My feet can stamp both in and out,
> In and out, in and out...
>
> My head can turn both right and left,
> Right and left, right and left...

Encourage the children to join in with the movements. For the first verse, clap up high in the air and then clap down low near the ground. For the second verse, stamp forwards and backwards. For the third verse, the head should turn slowly, but do not worry if the children muddle up their left and their right! Exaggerate your movements, so that the children can follow you.

When the children have learned the song, at the end of each verse call out an instruction, for example: 'Clap five times!'. Then, count together the numbers as the children clap the required amount.

Support and extension
This is a very simple action song in which the children can fully participate. Younger children may need more time to learn the actions to accompany the verses. Consider altering the rhyme for older children to introduce different actions, involving numbers and movements.

Further ideas
■ Make a collection of other action rhymes, such as, 'This Little Piggy', 'Round and Round the Garden', 'Ring-a-Ring o' Roses', 'Hokey Cokey' and so on.
■ Make a long crocodile and follow one another's movements. Repeat the movements a set number of times. Ask the children questions, such as, 'How many times did we clap our hands?'

Patterns and structures

This chapter helps to focus on the structure of the counting system. The activities will encourage the children to sustain interest, talk about, recognise and recreate simple patterns, use everyday words to describe postion and develop mathematical ideas to solve problems.

Colouring the teddies

What you need
Colour dice or spinner; coloured pens; scissors; the photocopiable sheet 'Teddies on the wall' on page 75.

Preparation
Make enough copies of the photocopiable sheet 'Teddies on the wall' so that there is one for each child.

What to do
Give a copy of the photocopiable sheet, 'Teddies on the wall', to each child. Invite each child to roll the colour dice and colour in one teddy to match the colour thrown. Continue with each child taking turns to roll the dice. During the activity ask the children questions, such as, 'How many teddies have you coloured in green (blue, red and so on)?', 'How many different colours have you used?', 'Did anyone use five different colours?' and 'Which colour is your first (last) teddy?'.

When all the teddies have been coloured, cut along the lines as marked and ask the children to fold down a specific coloured teddy (for example, a blue teddy, yellow teddy and so on). Can all the children fold down a teddy? Who has folded down the most teddies?

Support and extension
For younger children, limit the dice and pens to three different colours. For older children, modify one of the faces of the dice to be multicoloured, so that the children have a choice of colours.

Further ideas
■ Number the teddies with numerals or dots. Ask the children to roll a number dice, as well as the colour dice, to indicate which teddy should be coloured in which colour. In this version of the game, if the child rolls a number for a teddy already coloured in, they could either roll again or miss a turn. Rolling a six, could either mean that the child can choose a colour, or roll the dice again.
■ See also the activity 'Five brown teddies' on page 36.

LEARNING OBJECTIVES
STEPPING STONE
Use some number names and number language spontaneously.

EARLY LEARNING GOAL
Use developing mathematical ideas and methods to solve practical problems.

GROUP SIZE
Small group.

HOME LINKS
Ask parents if their children can bring in a selection of their soft toys from home. Sort them into sets of teddies and 'not teddies'.

Teddy patterns

What you need
A set of small bears, such as Three Bears Family or Compare Bears.

Preparation
To help the children focus on the colour patterns, decide on a particular size of bear and remove the others.

What to do
Let the children handle the bears, so that they are aware of their different colours. Ask the children to make sets of coloured bears (such as, a set of blue bears, yellow bears and so on). Working as a group, count the number of bears in each set.

Once you are satisfied that the children are familiar with the different colours, show them a pattern of bears (such as, blue, yellow, blue, yellow, blue, yellow and so on). Challenge the children in the group to continue the pattern.

Experiment with different repeating patterns, perhaps blue, blue, green, blue, blue, green, blue, blue. Can the children work out which colour bear is next?

Ask the children to look away and, while they are not looking, remove a bear. Can the children work out which bear is missing?

Support and extension
For younger children, confine the patterns to only two different colours. Ask questions based on continuing the pattern and finding a missing bear. For older children, the activity can be extended to include bears of two different sizes (for example, large and small). Make up a pattern using the same colour bears but varying the size. Then, try patterns based both on size and colour.

Further ideas
■ Make up a simple, two-colour pattern. Can the children continue the pattern to find the colour of the tenth or twentieth bear?
■ It is also possible to use Linking Elephants or Camels, instead of the bears.

I'm the leader!

What you need
Just the children.

What to do
Ask the children to stand in a line facing you. Decide on a particular movement, such as hops or jumps, and ask the children to copy your movements exactly. If you jump three times, the children should jump three times too.

Start with fairly simple movements (two jumps, one hop and so on) and check that the children are counting and copying you correctly.

Then, when the children are familiar and confident with the activity, begin to include sequences of movements, such as two jumps followed by four claps. Ask individual children to say how many times you jumped, clapped and so on.

Invite a child to come out of the line and to face the other children. Encourage them to make up a simple sequence of movements for the rest of the children to copy.

Support and extension
With younger children, introduce the activity in a small group. Also count aloud your number of jumps, as you do them and then again with the children. For older children, incorporate a longer sequence of movements.

Further ideas
■ Use number cards to indicate how many jumps or hops. Call out a child, secretly show them a number card and ask them to hop (jump, clap and so on) that number of times. Can the rest of the group work out the number written on the card?
■ Challenge the children to make up a dance of repeating movements to move around the room.
■ Sit the children in a circle. Ask the first child to stand, the second to sit and so on, to make a simple repeating pattern.

Magic circles

What you need
The photocopiable sheet 'Magic shapes' on page 76; scissors; card; coloured pens; magic wand (optional).

Preparation
Make two copies of the photocopiable sheet on page 76 on to card. On one copy, cut out the three rectangles and fold along the centre line. The shapes can be coloured if wished. Cut out the other copy into six individual squares.

What to do
Tell the children that you are going to perform some magic tricks! Show them the folded rectangle cards Explain that you will be able to tell them the number of circles on both sides, having only seen one side of the card!

Select a child to choose one of the 'squares' and to show you only one side of it. Think hard, perhaps tapping the card with your magic wand, and then say how many circles are on the other side. Each card adds up to five, so if there are four circles on one side, the other will have one circle.

The children will be amazed as you will be able to repeat the trick using the other two cards!

Repeat the activity, this time asking the children to guess how you were able to perform the 'magic trick.' Encourage the children to think about the total number of circles seen on both sides of the square. Explain that if they see four circles on one side of the square, they need to work out how many circles, hidden on the other side, would make five: $4 + ... = 5$.

Support and extension
For younger children, make use of the cut-out card squares. If you choose a square card with two circles on it, can they find the matching card which will show a total of five circles? Encourage older children to do the 'magic trick' in front of the group.

Further ideas
■ Invite the children to design their own set of magic cards and then perform their 'tricks'!
■ Consider asking the children to create another set to explore combinations totalling six or seven.

Shouts and whispers!

What you need
Just the children.

What to do
Invite the children to sit in a circle on the carpet. Tell them that they are going to play a game where the children have to either shout or whisper their name. Ask individual children to demonstrate by either shouting or whispering their names.

Explain that it would be very noisy if everyone shouted or whispered at the same time, so they will need to work in sequence and that you will start, followed by the child on your immediate right and so on, round the circle. The pattern will be: shout, whisper, shout, whisper and so on.

Start the pattern by shouting aloud your name, followed by the child on your right whispering their name. Continue in this way until everyone has either shouted or whispered their name.

Repeat the process but, this time, start by whispering your name, so that the children who previously shouted are now whispering their name.

Support and extension
For younger children, work in small groups. With older children, try extending the game by standing the group in a line, rather than sitting in a circle. If they shout their name out, then they must sit down, but, if they whisper, they remain standing.

Further ideas
■ Rather than shouting or whispering their names, the children could count in order, with odd numbers being shouted and even numbers whispered.
■ Add body movements to the pattern sequence, such as, jumping and not jumping, hopping and not hopping, and so on.
■ Consider incorporating clapping and clicking sequences, for example, shout and clap, whisper and click fingers.
■ With the children sitting in a circle, use a selection of musical instruments to make up different repeating patterns.

LEARNING OBJECTIVES
STEPPING STONE
Sustain interest for a length of time on a pre-decided construction or arrangement.

EARLY LEARNING GOAL
Talk about, recognise and re-create simple patterns.

GROUP SIZE
Large group.

HOME LINKS
Suggest that parents play question and answer games with their children at home, based on shouting the question and then whispering the answer. Who forgets first is out of the game.

Who has the most?

What you need
Counters or similar for counting purposes.

What to do
Explain to the children that they are going to count in order, each person saying one number in sequence, for example: if you start by saying one, the next child says two, the next, three, but limiting the counting up to four. The fifth person begins the sequence again at one. Continue playing the game in this way.

Once the children are confident with this activity, explain that the person who says 'three' must pick up three counters. Repeat the counting round a few more times and then ask the children to count how many counters they have. Ask, who has the most counters? Who has the least counters? Has anyone only three counters? Has anyone more than nine counters?

Show the children how to compare the number of counters two children have collected, by laying them in two columns alongside one another. The longest column should be very apparent.

A winner can be declared as the first person to collect nine counters!

Support and extension
Younger children can collect two counters each time the number two is said. For older children, consider expanding both the group size and counting round, and perhaps collecting counters when both the number names three and five are said!

Further ideas
■ Recite the number names in order, but start at six and descend down to zero!

■ Find out who has the most counters in the group, by laying all the counters in columns to find the longest counter column. Who has the shortest column?

■ Give each child six counters and, this time, when the number three is said, discard rather than collect three counters. Who is the first to 'lose' all their counters?

LEARNING OBJECTIVES

STEPPING STONE
Say the number after any number up to 9.

EARLY LEARNING GOAL
Say and use number names in order in familiar contexts.

GROUP SIZE
Five or more children.

HOME LINKS
Ask parents if they can teach their children a singing round: that is, the parent and child sing the same song, but at different intervals. Much practice is required! Suggest that parents help their children to practise counting at home, for example, cutlery into a drawer, toys in the cupboard and so on.

Noisy counting!

What you need
Just the children.

What to do
Invite the children to sit in a circle. Explain to the children that they are going to count in order, but, instead of saying the number out loud, each child should choose an animal sound and make the appropriate number of noises to represent that number name. For example, the first child barks once, the second child miaows twice, the third child grunts three times and so on, up to five. The sixth child chooses a new animal sound to re-start the counting process, beginning at one again.

Once all the children are familiar with the activity, start counting down from five to one, in the same way, letting the children decide on the animal noises they want to make.

As the children gain confidence, extend the counting up to ten and then back down to one.

Support and extension
For younger children, simplify the sound pattern by choosing and repeating only two different noises, for example, one bark, two quacks, three barks, four quacks. For older children, rather than counting round a circle, point to a child, at random, to begin at one and then at another to count two and so on, up to ten.

Further ideas
■ Link this activity to the singing game 'Old McDonald' had a farm on page 34. Ask the group to agree on a target number, such as five. Count as before, around the group, starting from one. When ten is reached start counting again from one. Any child who says the target number is out of the game. Who will be the winner?
■ With all the children sitting in a circle, invite the first child to clap once, the second child to shake their head twice, the third child claps three times and so on.

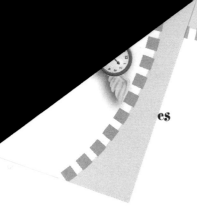

Post-it numbers

What you need
Post-it Notes (or similar); pencil; rope or large hoops to form sets.

What to do
Write the numbers '1', '2' or '3' on each Post-it Note and stick one on to the front of each child's jumper. Ask the children to respond to your instructions based on the number written on their Post-it Note. Ask, for example, for all the children with the number 1 on their label to stand by the door; all the children with 3 written on their label to sit down; all the children with 2 written on their label to hop on one leg, and so on.

Then, form sets, using either the rope shaped as a circle or the large playground hoops. Ask the children to stand in these sets if the number on their Post-it Note is less than 2, if their number is more than 2, their number is between 1 and 3, and so on. Continue in this way, using terms such as, 'next', 'between', 'before', 'after', 'one less than' and 'one more than'.

Support and extension
If younger children have difficulty recognising the written numerals, 1, 2, or 3, use dots to represent the numbers. Alternatively, different coloured Post-it Notes could be used to represent the numbers. For older children, extend the sequence to five and then perhaps up to ten.

Further ideas
■ Write a number between one and ten on a Post-it Note and stick it to a child's back, so that the other children can see it. The group has to give the child clues about the number written on the label, without using its name. They could say, for example: 'It is less than six' or, 'It is between two and four'. Can the child guess the number?

■ Ask the children to make up matching pairs. Can they pair up with another child with the same number on their label?

■ Invite the children to pair up, so that the numbers on both their labels add up to make six.

A handful of patterns

What you need
Just the children.

What to do
With the children sitting around a table, explain that they are going to make simple patterns using their hands. First, encourage the children to look closely at their hands, counting the number of fingers and then, folding down one finger at a time as they count up to five.

Next, show the children how to place their hand, palm side down, on the table top. Invite the first child to place five fingers, palm side down, on the table top, second child to place ten fingers, palm side down, the third child five fingers.

Ask the children if they can see the pattern – if so, what comes next?

Continue to form different patterns, such as palm up, palm down; four fingers then five fingers. You might even consider incorporating hands and feet!

Support and extension
For younger children, initially limit the patterns to using only one hand – perhaps a thumbs-up, thumbs-down pattern, using either right or left hand. Encourage older children to use both hands and all ten fingers.

Further ideas
■ Invite two children to hide their hands behind their back. Then ask the children to re-show their hands holding up some of their fingers (limit this up to five at first). Count and compare the number of fingers held up, for instance, 'Daniel is holding up one finger, Sally is holding up three fingers – Daniel is holding up fewer fingers than Sally'.
■ Make a handprint tree, by painting the children's hands and printing them on paper. Cut these out and glue to form a tree.
■ Compare a child's handprint to that of an adult. Whose is the biggest?

Bug patterns

What you need
Card (A4 size); the photocopiable sheet 'Bug cards' on page 68; scissors; colouring materials.

Preparation
Copy the photocopiable sheet on to the card to make a set of at least six of each bug card. Make up a zero bug card, by cutting up card to the same size, but leaving it blank.

What to do
Show the bug cards to the children and count together the number of bugs on each card.

Explain to the children that you are going to make a pattern with the cards. Emphasise that you want them to look at the pattern very carefully and predict the next card in the sequence. Place a bug card with one bug on it on the table

top, then a two bug card, followed by a one bug card and another two bug card. Can the children see a pattern? What card do they think should go next?

Repeat with other patterns, such as, one bug, three bugs, one bug, three bugs, and so on.

As the children gain in confidence, extend the patterns to using three bug cards, for instance: two bug, three bugs, one bug, two bugs, three bugs, one bug.

Throughout the activity use positional language, such as, 'next to', 'before', 'after' and 'beside'.

Ask one of the children to create a pattern with the cards. Can the group recognise the pattern?

Support and extension
For younger children, initially limit the patterns to two-card variations. With older children, consider introducing the zero card to allow for new patterns to be made, such as: zero bug card, three bugs, one bug, zero bug card, three bugs, one bug, zero bug card, three bugs, one bug.

Further ideas
■ Make up a pattern with the bug cards, and then ask the children to close their eyes as you remove a card. Can the children spot the 'mistake'?
■ Let the children colour in the bug cards, using one colour for each card. Make up patterns based on colour and number of bugs.

**LEARNING
OBJECTIVES
STEPPING STONE**
Observe and use positional language.

**EARLY LEARNING
GOAL**
Talk about, recognise and re-create simple patterns.

GROUP SIZE
Small group.

HOME LINKS
Ask parents to help their children look for, and sort, patterned objects at home, such as, cushions, clothes, toys and so on. Invite the children to bring in some patterned objects to show to the rest of the group.

Measures

Through these activities children will begin to use language to compare quantities and order items by weight, length and size. They will recognise some numerals of personal significance, and learn to choose suitable components to build a model and sustain an interest in its construction.

How many fit in?

What you need
Selection of plastic containers, such as those used for water/sand play, ensuring that at least two of the containers are the same (for example, plastic cups); small items, such as LEGO blocks, cotton reels, Compare Bears, felt-tipped pens; labels.

What to do
Show the containers to the children and discuss how they are usually filled with water or sand. Explain that, this time, they are going to filled with the small items. Show the children your various small items.

Ask the children how many blocks (for example) they think will fit into the plastic cup. Then fill the cup with blocks, counting as they are placed in it.

Refill the cup with another type of small item, such as the cotton reels or bears. How many will fill the cup? Is it more or less than the number of blocks? Rather than using the same cup to be filled and emptied, it would be advantageous to have several identical cups and allow the children to 'see' the cups filled with blocks, reels, Compare Bears.

Make labels to indicate how many fitted into the containers, for example: ten blocks filled the cup; eight bears filled the cup, and so on.

Support and extension
Let younger children compare two different-sized containers filled with the same item. Which holds most and which holds least? For older children, use different-sized containers and different small items, but be careful not to use very small items for filling purposes as this would exceed the children's counting sequence.

Further ideas
■ Link this game to activities based on measures. Compare a container filled with sand or water to a container filled with blocks.
■ Make use of the correct terms, for example, 'full', 'half full', 'empty'.

Teddy ruler

What you need
Set of Compare Bears (using only the large bears); pieces of card to make rulers; pencil; marker pen; scissors; coloured pens; various items for measuring (such as, pencils, blocks, toy cars, books); the photocopiable sheet 'Teddy ruler' on page 77.

Preparation
Enlarge the photocopiable sheet on page 77 to A3 size.

What to do
Explain to the children that they are going to make a teddy ruler. Ask them to count out five bears and position them on the card, so that they touch one another lengthways. Mark this length on the card – this is their five-bear ruler. Cut out these lengths for the children and let them add decorations if they wish, such as drawing faces and clothes on the teddies. Show the children how to use their teddy ruler to find items which are longer or shorter than it, by comparing the ruler to the various small items placed on the table top.

Teach the children how to use the teddy ruler correctly, by positioning the ruler at the edge of the item to be measured and then comparing the length of each object. Sort the items on the table top into those which are shorter than, the same size as, and longer than the five-bear ruler. The various sizes could be recorded, using the photocopiable sheet (enlarged to A3 size) as a chart, and positioning the items in the correct categories.

The sheet could also be used as a group recording activity, by drawing pictures of the items compared to the ruler.

Support and extension
The children could use bear stamps to make rulers of different lengths, perhaps limiting the number of bears to three for younger children, but extending up to ten bears for older children.

Further ideas
■ Challenge the children to find five items which are longer than the five-bear ruler, then five items which are shorter, and five that are the same size.
■ Extend the activity to note how items can be both longer and shorter, depending on the length of ruler used to measure it, for example, 'My reading book is longer than the eight-bear ruler, but shorter than the 20-bear ruler'.

The biggest hand!

What you need
Items to count such as, teddy-bear, elephant or camel counters, toy wooden bricks, shells, pine cones; paper; marker pens.

What to do
Explain to the children that you are all going to try and find out who has the largest hand. Ask the children for suggestions of ways to do this.

Discuss the ideas, such as observing everyone's hands closely and placing the hands, palm to palm. Let the children try out the palm to palm idea so they realise how difficult it is to find the biggest hand!

Then, invite the children to try and find the largest hand by drawing around their hand and seeing how many different items they can place on the hand outline.

Give each child in the group a sheet of paper and help them to use the pen to draw around their hand.

Let the children experiment by placing different items all over their hand outline. Ask them to count up the objects – can they now find out who has the biggest hand? Remember to compare hand size fairly, the same items must be used to cover all the outlines!

Support and extension
With younger children, use fairly large items to fit on their hand outline. This will make the counting process easier. Challenge older children to cover their hand outlines with different items and then compare the amounts such as, 'Nine elephant counters will fit on my hand and if I use coloured counters I can fit 12 on my hand'.

Further ideas
■ Invite the children to investigate how many different items they can grab with their hand.
■ Ask the children to try to cover their hand completely using ten items, then only eight items and so on.

Stride out!

LEARNING OBJECTIVES

STEPPING STONE
Sometimes show confidence and offer solutions to problems.

EARLY LEARNING GOAL
Use language such as 'more' or 'less' to compare two numbers.

GROUP SIZE
Large group.

What you need
Beanbags.

What to do
Invite the children to sit in a circle. Ask one child to stand up in the centre of the circle and then to guess how many steps it will take to reach you. Emphasise that you do not expect a 'right' answer, the aim is to 'estimate'. When the child has made their guess, let them slowly step towards you, counting out loud. Ask the child to say again how many steps they thought it would take and how many it actually took. Was it more or less? Repeat the activity several times, asking different children to walk from various starting to finishing points. Then, place two beanbags at two different points. Ask three children to step from one beanbag to the other, each using a different length of step. One child should take 'baby' steps, another, normal-sized steps and the

third, 'giant' steps. Who will need most steps and who will need the least steps? Can the children explain why? Complete the game by counting, as a whole group, the number of steps the three children take. Compare the results by asking relevant questions.

Support and extension
With younger children it may be appropriate to use only two different types of steps – little steps and big steps. With older children, try lengthening the gap between the two beanbags and comparing different types of movements, such as three different jumps, three different hops and so on.

Further ideas
■ Link the activity to acting out traditional stories, such as 'Goldilocks and the Three Bears', 'The Three Billy Goats Gruff' and 'Jack and the Beanstalk'.
■ Use the different movements within the children's dance sessions, by asking them all to stride out like a giant and to take little baby steps!

HOME LINKS
Ask parents to help their children compare the different pace lengths of an adult and a child.

Happy birthday!

What you need
A selection of used or new birthday cards, showing various ages on the front.

What to do
Start by asking the children questions about their age, such as how old they are and the date, or just the month or season, of their birthday. Then, discuss their birthday parties, asking questions about the games played, the type of cake, the number of candles on the cake, the presents and birthday cards.

Show one of the birthday cards and ask the children to guess how old they think the child might have been when they received that particular card. Is there a clue on the card? Draw their attention to the numeral written on the front of the card – ask the children which numeral it is, and if any of them are that age.

Bring out the other cards and ask the children to pick up a card for a child who will be three and will be four, cards with badges, and so on.

Look at the cards in greater detail, such as a pink, princess card, would they send this card to a boy or a girl?

Depending on the range of cards available, ask the children to arrange them in order from their first birthday card to their sixth birthday card.

Encourage the children to find different ways of making sets with the cards. (This might be different ages, cards with and without badges, cards based on a television programme, and so on.)

Support and extension
For younger children, limit the number of cards to be sorted, but encourage the children to bring their old birthday cards to show the rest of the group. Encourage older children to use the cards to make a number line, by positioning the cards in order from 1 to 10.

Further ideas
■ Make a birthday cake and have a party!
■ Collect together 'times ten' birthday cards (for example, 10, 20, 30 and so on). Can the children arrange these in order?

LEARNING OBJECTIVES
STEPPING STONE
Recognise some numerals of personal significance.

EARLY LEARNING GOAL
Use developing mathematical ideas and methods to solve practical problems.

GROUP SIZE
Small group.

HOME LINKS
Ask parents to let their children bring in used birthday cards from home. Invite the children to make a birthday card for a family member – which numerals should they write on the card?

How tall are you?

LEARNING OBJECTIVES

STEPPING STONE
Choose suitable components to make a particular model.

EARLY LEARNING GOAL
Use developing mathematical ideas and methods to solve practical problems.

GROUP SIZE
Large or small group.

What you need
Variety of different materials to make up a child's height, such as large plastic bricks, small interlocking cubes, empty boxes including shoeboxes and cereal boxes, as well as a few larger ones collected from a supermarket.

Preparation
Collect a set of suitable large materials which you can use to measure the height of each child.

What to do
Invite the children to sit in a large circle. Ask who is the tallest child in the group. Accept their various answers and explain that they are going to try and find out how tall each person is by measuring their height using different materials.

Show the children a variety of different materials, such as small cubes, large wooden blocks, plastic bricks, empty shoeboxes and so on. Ask them if they think they should measure their height using the small cubes or large plastic bricks. Can the children give a valid reason for their choice of materials?

Choose a child to stand by the wall and line up a range of suitable materials, so that they equal the child's height. Then ask the children to count with you the materials used, for example: 'Michael's height is equal to two cereal boxes, two shoeboxes and five large bricks'.

Continue until each child has had a turn.

Support and extension
For younger children, rather than measuring their height, consider measuring the length of their arm, their hand or their leg. Older children can try to measure their heights in different ways, such as, four cereal boxes and two large blocks, or three cereal boxes and four blocks and one small brick.

Further ideas
■ Challenge the children to measure their height using ten different items.
■ Invite the children to cut strips of paper to match the length of their shoe or foot. Then, ask them to find out how many interlocking cubes it takes to make a line the same length as the strip of paper. Whose line of cubes is the longest (shortest)? Who has the biggest (smallest) foot?

HOME LINKS
Suggest that the children find out who is the tallest in their house. Ask parents to help their children arrange the family in order of height from the shortest to the tallest.

How much does it weigh?

What you need
Selection of different items of fruit and/or vegetables (do not use items which are too heavy to weigh); bucket scales; interlocking blocks or similar to use as 'weights'.

What to do
Let the children choose a piece of fruit or vegetable. Place the chosen piece in one of the buckets of the balance scales and gradually count aloud any suitable non-standard unit, such as interlocking blocks, into the other bucket until the scales balance.

Tip out the blocks and count again their total. Encourage the children to say with you, for example, 'Eight blocks balance the apple'.

Continue to weigh a variety of different fruit and vegetables. Ensure that the non-standard unit used to weigh the fruit or vegetables is not too small and light, as too many will be required to balance the items, which may cause counting difficulties.

When several items have been weighed, discuss which fruit or vegetable was the heaviest (needed the most blocks to balance the scales) and which was the lightest (needed the least blocks to balance the scales).

Support and extension
For younger children use plastic zoo animals rather than fruit and vegetables, so that the number of non-standard units needed to balance the scales is manageable. Challenge older children to order three items of fruit or vegetables from the heaviest to the lightest and vice versa, and find two items that weigh just about the same.

Further ideas
■ Ask two children to choose an item of fruit each and to decide which they think is the heaviest and which is the lightest. They can then compare them by using the bucket scales.

■ Ask the children to choose one piece of fruit and then to find another, which is either heavier or lighter than their chosen item.
■ How heavy is a pumpkin? Investigate!
■ Challenge the children to find out how many grapes weigh the same as ten interlocking blocks.

LEARNING OBJECTIVES
STEPPING STONE
Order two items by weight or capacity.

EARLY LEARNING GOAL
Use language such as 'greater', 'smaller', 'heavier' or 'lighter' to compare quantities.

GROUP SIZE
Any size.

HOME LINKS
Ask parents to help their children use a weighing scale to weigh ingredients to make a cake.

In a minute!

LEARNING OBJECTIVES

STEPPING STONE

Sustain interest for a length of time on a pre-decided construction or arrangement.

EARLY LEARNING GOAL

Use developing mathematical ideas and methods to solve practical problems.

GROUP SIZE

Small group.

What you need

A minute sand-timer or a clock or watch with the minute markings; large plastic needles threaded with thick wool or string, or suitable long shoe laces. Materials for threading (such as foil bottle tops, pieces of card, cut-up egg-boxes, buttons, beads and so on); interlocking blocks (LEGO or DUPLO).

What to do

Discuss with the children the different parts of the day, using vocabulary associated to time, such as, morning, night, afternoon. Ask the children what other similar words they know.

Tell the children that time is measured using common words such as an hour and a minute. Again, ask if the children have heard these words and discuss their meaning.

Explain that the children are going to try and do different things in the short period of time called a minute. Show the children the sand-timer and explain how it works, or alternatively, show them the clock.

Discuss what the children could do in a minute and then suggest they try out some different activities, such as how many items (bottle tops, cut-out egg-boxes and so on) they can thread on a string in one minute.

After the minute, encourage the children to count the threaded items and see who, in the group, threaded the most items.

Then, challenge the children to find out how many block towers they can build in a minute. Count the number of blocks used in the different towers to find out which is the tallest tower. How high a tower can the children build working as a group of four or in a pairs in a minute?

Support and extension

It will help both younger and older children to practise this activity, but assist the younger children more than the older children. Perhaps older children could be set specific patterns, such as alternating colours in the block towers.

Further idea

■ Working as a large group, try out other things you can do in a minute such as: jumping, hopping, counting and taking off shoes and socks!

HOME LINKS

Ask parents to show their children different clocks and timers. Ask them to 'time' their children during specified activities such as brushing their teeth.

Shape and space

The activities in this chapter will enable children to recognise the differences between 3-D and 2-D shapes using mathematical terms. They will begin to position and match shapes by recognising similarities and orientation and show curiosity and observation through talking about shapes.

Hold up your flag if...

What you need
Lolly sticks or straws; assorted paper shapes or paper which varies in shape and colour; sticky tape; marker pen; coloured pens; scissors; glue.

Preparation
Make a set of ten shape flags, by attaching a piece of paper on to a lolly stick or similar. Use paper in different shapes and colours or draw or glue a different shape on to the paper. Make sure you produce a good variety of shapes and colours.

What to do
Show the children the ten shape flags and discuss their different colours, sizes and shapes. Give out the ten flags – one each to ten children.

Explain that these children must hold their flag up high if their shape matches the instructions you are going to call out. Say, for example, 'Hold up your flag if your shape is a circle', 'Hold up your flag if it is coloured blue' and so on.

After a while, when you are confident that the chidren have understood what to do, take the flags and re-distribute them to another ten children. Continue the activity, asking once more the children to hold up their flags following your instuctions.

Support and extension
For younger children, use shapes which differ either in colour or shape only. Challenge older children to respond to more complex requests, such as; 'Hold your flag up if your shape is a triangle, but not blue'.

Further ideas
■ Progress to more complex instructions, for example, begin by asking the children to hold up their flag if their shape is a square. Then, continue by asking them to show you three squares. Now, some of the children who held up their flags, as squares, may need to lower them, so that there are only three squares held up.
■ Consider showing the children flags representing different countries. Ask the children to spot the different shapes and colours in these flags.

LEARNING OBJECTIVES
STEPPING STONE
Begin to use mathematical names for 'solid' 3-D shapes and 'flat' 2-D shapes and mathematical terms to describe shapes.

EARLY LEARNING GOAL
Use developing mathematical ideas and methods to solve practical problems.

GROUP SIZE
Whole group.

HOME LINKS
Ask parents to help their children look for square, circle, triangle and rectangle shapes at home or on a walk. Challenge them to find at least one different object for the four basic shapes. Suggest that parents point out different flags seen locally to their children, such as flags used to promote different events.

Shape lotto

What you need

The photocopiable sheet 'Lotto game' on page 78; shape dice; scissors; colouring crayons (optional).

Preparation

Prepare the lotto boards by photocopying page 78. Leave some of the sheets whole as a base board and cut some up to make individual shape cards. Colour in the shapes – optional.

What to do

Give each child a four-shape lotto board. Discuss and name the shapes that they can see on their boards.

Count the total number of shapes and draw the children's attention to the number of sides of each shape. Ask the children to place their finger on the shape with three sides, four sides and so on. How many sides has the circle?

Show the individual shape cards and place these face down in the middle of the table. Tell the children that they are each going to turn over the top card and, if this card matches a shape on their board, they can match it by placing it on their base board. The game continues in this fashion until a child has covered all four shapes and shouts out 'Lotto!'.

Support and extension

It would assist younger children if the shapes both on the base board and on the individual cards had been coloured in, to make the cards easier to match up. Extend the game for older children by using a six-shape board. In this version of the game, still use the basic four shapes, repeat two in different sizes or colours. The children need to look carefully at their boards to match the cards for shape and colour, or even shape, colour and size.

Further ideas

- A shape dice can be used, rather than turning over cards.
- Play the game in reverse, by starting with the cards on the base board. Invite the children to roll the shape dice to indicate which cards to remove. The winner is the first to discard all their shape cards.

LEARNING OBJECTIVES

STEPPING STONE
Match some shapes by recognising similarities and orientation.

EARLY LEARNING GOAL
Use everyday words to describe position.

GROUP SIZE
Up to four children.

HOME LINKS
Give parents a copy of the game, so that they can play it at home with their children. Suggest that the children try to make a shape game of their own at home.

Disappearing stars

What you need
The photocopiable sheet 'Folding stars' on page 79; coloured crayons; scissors; marker pen.

Preparation
Prepare the star by copying the photocopiable sheet on page 79. Crease along the dotted lines as indicated, so that the points can be folded. The smaller stars on the points can be coloured in, if you so wish.

What to do
Show the children the star. Count the number of points on the star and then count the smaller stars on the points, both as individual totals and as a grand total of ten.

Ensure the children realise that the number of stars on each point varies from zero to four. Ask the children which point has the smallest number of stars and which has the most stars. Then, ask which points have more than one star and which have less than three stars.

Fold in one of the points of the star, thus hiding some of the smaller stars. Ask the children how many small stars have disappeared. Encourage the children to look at the other open points of the star and to try and remember which amount is missing, rather than just guessing.

Repeat the activity, folding in different points.

Support and extension
To simplify the star for younger children, draw one star in the zero section. It is also possible to write the corresponding numerals on the reverse of the star, so, when a point is folded in, the children can see the number of missing stars. For older children, two points could be folded in at the same time. Then the children have to work out a combined amount of missing stars!

Further ideas
■ The total number of stars drawn on the points could be decreased or increased to make the activity easier or more difficult.
■ Give the star to one of the children and ask them to fold in a point which has three stars, and so on.
■ Practise number bonds to ten using the star.

LEARNING OBJECTIVES
STEPPING STONE
Show an interest in number problems.

EARLY LEARNING GOAL
Use language such as 'more' or 'less' to compare two numbers.

GROUP SIZE
Four to six children.

HOME LINKS
On a clear night, suggest that parents might show their children the stars in the sky. Suggest that the children make a star collage at home, by cutting out star shapes from newspapers and magazines.

Finger flip-flap

What you need
Pieces of paper 20cm x 20cm (that is the largest square made from a sheet of A4); marker pen; small gummed shapes (optional).

Preparation
Make a finger flip-flap using a square sheet of paper. Fold in all four corners to the centre point of the square, then turn over the sheet and again fold in each corner to the centre point. Once you turn the paper over, you can now insert your fingers into the four flaps, so that the paper can be opened and closed rather like a mouth!

What to do
Show the children the paper flip-flap and demonstrate how you can insert your fingers into the flaps to make the mouth open and close!

Using the marker pen write the numerals 1 to 4 on the front four flaps. Then, on the inside eight triangle flaps, draw different shapes or use the small gummed shapes. Lift these triangular flaps and write out eight different instructions, such as, jump up and down three times, clap four times, nod your head two times and, hop five times.

Insert your fingers into the front flaps and ask a child to chose a number from one to four, then open and close the 'mouth' that many times.

Ask the child to chose a shape, lift up the flap and read out the task. The child must then obey the instruction that is given.

Repeat the game, asking other children in the group to choose their starting number, shape and then to complete the given instruction.

Support and extension
For younger children, rather than writing the numerals, dots could be used to represent the numbers. For older children, consider increasing the numbers written on finger flip-flap or the number of repeats of the different instructions.

Further ideas
■ Vary the options on the flaps and written instructions.
■ Let the children make their own finger flip-flaps.

LEARNING OBJECTIVES
STEPPING STONE
Count actions or objects that cannot be moved.

EARLY LEARNING GOAL
Recognise numerals 1 to 9.

GROUP SIZE
Small group.

HOME LINKS
Show parents how to make the finger flip-flap, so that they can make and use it at home. Suggest that parents help their children to think up other ideas for instructions to go inside their finger flip-flap.

Tower patterns

What you need
Interlocking blocks (such as LEGO or DUPLO); Linking Elephants; colour dice.

Preparation
Make a pattern using ten interlocking blocks, such as blue, yellow, blue, yellow and so on.

What to do
Show the children the patterned tower that you have created using the ten blocks. Ask the children to count the number of blocks in your pattern and to describe the pattern that you have made.

Ask the children to build their own patterned tower.

Give the children a few minutes to decide on their colours and then to build their tower. When they have finished, question them on their use of pattern and the number of blocks used. Ask, for example, 'Can you explain your pattern?', 'Does the pattern have any mistakes?', 'How many blocks did you use?'. Now, say that they are going to make another tower, but this time they will make it differently! Invite the children, in turn, to roll the colour dice two times. This will decide the two different colours to be used in their pattern.

Then, ask the children to build their towers, encouraging them to experiment with different patterns, such as blue, blue, yellow, rather than just alternating the colours. Suggest that the children use a colour dice with a 1, 1, 2, 2, 3, 3 dice. First they roll the colour dice, followed by the number dice, to create their pattern. So they might throw: blue, 3; green, 1; red, 2.

Support and extension
Help younger children to 'spot' the pattern, perhaps by starting a tower and letting them complete it. Challenge older children to make towers which are a specific number of blocks in height, such as a 12-tower, or to incorporate more complex patterns within their towers.

Further ideas
■ Use the Linking Elephants to make patterns which the children are able to link together to form a complete circle. Question them about the start and end of the pattern!

■ Challenge the children to predict which colour the thirteenth block in their pattern would be. Ask them to explain their reasoning.

■ Build a patterned tower, but make a mistake in the pattern. Can the children spot it?

Musical shapes

What you need
Different coloured sugar paper; tape recorder and suitable musical tape.

Preparation
Using the sugar paper, cut out large paper shapes, several each of squares, rectangles, circles and triangles.

What to do
Show the children the paper cut-outs and point out the attributes of the different shapes. Ask questions using mathematical terms, such as, how many straight sides, how many corners, which is the longest (shortest) and so on. Ask a child to walk around a shape, counting the number of sides and corners.

Arrange five or more paper cut-outs on the floor, ensuring that there is sufficient space between each shape. Start with the same number of children as there are shapes, that is, one shape per child. Play the music and when the music stops the children must sit on any of the paper shapes but only one child on each shape. Take away one shape before the next turn. Continue to play the game.

The child without a paper shape to sit on, when the music stops, is out of the game. The winner is the last to be out. Alternatively, just play for fun! Repeat the game several times, so that all the children have a go.

If you wish you can alter the game, by asking each player, each time the music stops, to find and sit on a certain shape. If the shape is withdrawn, the child is out of the game!

Support and extension
The game can be made easier for younger children by using the same colour for the same shape (for example, all squares could be red). For older children, suggest standing, hopping or jumping on the allocated shape, rather than just sitting!

Further ideas
■ Unlike 'Musical chairs', the number of cut-outs do not have to be reduced, therefore, there does not necessarily have to be a winner or loser!
■ Rather than use shape names, tell the children to sit on shapes which have four sides, three sides, more than two sides, less than five sides, and so on.

Find this shape!

What you need

Large paper cut-outs of a square, circle, rectangle and triangle (see 'Musical shapes' on page 62); drawstring bag; set of 2-D shapes; set of 3-D shapes; the photocopiable sheet 'Shape labels' on page 80; number squares, 1 to 6, on the photocopiable sheet on page 69.

Preparation

Place the 2-D shapes in the drawstring bag. Copy the photocopiable sheet on page 80 for reference. Prepare the number squares, 1 to 6, on the photocopiable sheet on page 69.

What to do

Place the paper cut-out of a square on the table. Count its sides and discuss its different attributes using appropriate terms, such as those on the

photocopiable sheet on page 80. These terms encourage children to recognise the different properties of shapes towards the end of the reception year.

Explain that you have placed some 2-D shapes in the drawstring bag and the children must feel in the bag and take out a specified shape, such as the square. Tell the children that they cannot look in the bag, but must *feel* for the shape. Encourage them to think about the attributes of the chosen shape, for example, will the shape have straight edges? Play this game using the four basic shapes.

The activity can be repeated using 3-D shapes. Once again encourage the children to feel for the different properties of the shapes.

Support and extension

Encourage younger children to pick out certain attributes of a shape, rather than finding a specific shape, for instance, a shape that rolls, or a shape with straight edges. Ask older children to pick a number square card to 'decide' the number of faces or edges of the shape to be found in the bag.

Further ideas

■ Use the different terms noted on the labels to extend the children's understanding of the properties of the shapes.
■ Put a shape in the drawstring bag and tell the children they must guess which shape it is. They can ask questions, such as, 'Does it roll?'. You can answer only 'yes' or 'no'. Can the children work out which shape it is?

LEARNING OBJECTIVES

STEPPING STONE
Show curiosity and observation by talking about shapes, how they are the same or why some are different.

EARLY LEARNING GOAL
Use language such as 'circle' or 'bigger' to describe the shape and size of solids and flat shapes.

GROUP SIZE
Small group.

HOME LINKS
Suggest that parents play simple 'I spy' games with their children, based on the properties of different shapes. Ask parents to help their children find different shapes around the home.

Make a picture!

What you need
Coloured paper cut-outs of different 2-D shapes, such as triangles, rectangles, squares and circles – ensure a good variety of colour, shape and size; glue; plain paper.

What to do
Let the children examine the different paper shapes. Discuss the different colours, sizes and outlines. Count the number of straight and curved edges for each shape.

Invite the children to choose up to six different paper cut-outs and to use these shapes to make a house picture. Give the children time to experiment with different ideas. Encourage them to consider what shape would be best for the roof and what they could use for the front of the house. Then, ask them to think about which shapes to use for the doors and windows.

Compare the different houses made by the children, by counting the number of shapes used by individual children and discussing the different colours and sizes. Talk about how the shapes have been positioned and encourage the children to use terms, such as: 'next to', 'above', 'under', 'besides' and so on. Ask if all the houses look the same, what difference can they see?

Invite the children to glue their house shapes on paper to form a wall display.

Support and extension
For younger children, provide an outline of a house shape (a square or rectangle topped by a triangle), so all the children have to do is fill this in with corresponding shapes. Invite older children to make another house, asking them to consider if they would prefer to use different shape cut-outs this time.

Further Ideas
■ Display all the house pictures, writing underneath how many shapes the children used.
■ Ask the children to make a shape picture using five shape cut-outs. How many different pictures can they make?

Square pegs

What you need
Pegboards and pegs and/or multilink pegboards and multilink blocks; tissue paper; gummed paper shapes; paper; glue; scissors. Multilink pegboards are excellent to use with young children, as card can be placed under the see-through board to show different patterns for the children to copy.

What to do
Show the children the pegboards and let them play freely with the materials to create different patterns. Comment on the different patterns created by the children and then ask them to make a pattern with a straight line, with a curved line, with a wavy line and so on.

Begin a square outline on the pegboard by using two pegs of the same colour, pegging these slightly apart. Invite the children to join these using a straight line of pegs. Ask them to repeat this on the other side, so that the two opposite sides of the square have been completed. Count both lines of pegs and comment that their total is the same. Finally ask the children to join these lines together to form a complete outline of a square.

Let the children make another square using different coloured pegs. To assist, this time, place four pegs on the board to represent the four corners of the square. Encourage the children to say who, in the group, has made the smallest and largest square and who has used most and least pegs.

Support and extension
For younger children peg out the complete outline of the square and ask them to fill it in using different rows of colours. For older children, place the four pegs, for the corners of the square, in a diamond pattern. Can the children join these pegs to make a square?

Further ideas
■ Challenge the children to make any other shapes on their pegboards, such as triangles or rectangles.
■ When filling in the outline of the square, ask the children to consider different patterns of pegs (such as, rows or columns of different colours or symmetrical patterns).

LEARNING OBJECTIVES
STEPPING STONE
Show awareness of symmetry.

EARLY LEARNING GOAL
Talk about, recognise and re-create simple patterns.

GROUP SIZE
Small group.

HOME LINKS
Ask parents to help their children find square shaped objects at home. Suggest that the children make a simple collage of paper squares in different colours and sizes and bring it in to show the group.

Shape patterns

What you need
The photocopiable sheet, 'Shape lotto' on page 78; scissors; colouring pens.

Preparation
Make several copies of the photocopiable sheet and cut out the shapes to make individual shape cards. Colour them in using one colour for triangles, another for circles and so on.

What to do
Pick up two of the shape cards (such as a rectangle and triangle) and show these cards to the children. Ask the children to compare these two shapes and state what is the same and what is different about them, for instance: 'The triangle is blue', 'The rectangle is yellow', 'The triangle has three sides', 'The rectangle has four sides' and so on.

Make a repeating pattern, using these shape picture cards, such as: rectangle, triangle, rectangle, triangle. Discuss this pattern with the children. Ask which

is the first shape in the pattern and which is the second shape. Can the children predict which shape should follow the triangle? Start the process again, using two different shapes. First, compare the shapes and then use the appropriate cards to make up a repeating pattern.

Support and extension
If the assortment of shapes is too much for younger children, help them to sort out the two shape cards they want to use. Colouring all the shapes in the same colour will help. Encourage older children to make up patterns involving three different shapes or repeating patterns of a certain length for example, 12 cards.

Further ideas
■ Ask the children to copy a pattern that you have created.
■ Invite the children to continue a pattern that you have started.
■ Give the children a set number of shapes (such as, two circle cards and one triangle card). How many different patterns can they create?
■ Make up a six-shape pattern and then ask the children to predict what shape will be seventh, or twelfth.
■ Create a symmetrical pattern, by placing a square card in the centre and then placing two triangle cards either side of it. Continue to extend this pattern, by placing identical cards either end of the sequence.

Movement spinner

Photocopy on to card, cut out the spinner and insert a pencil in the middle to make it spin. Use with a dice so that the child's actions correspond with the number thrown.

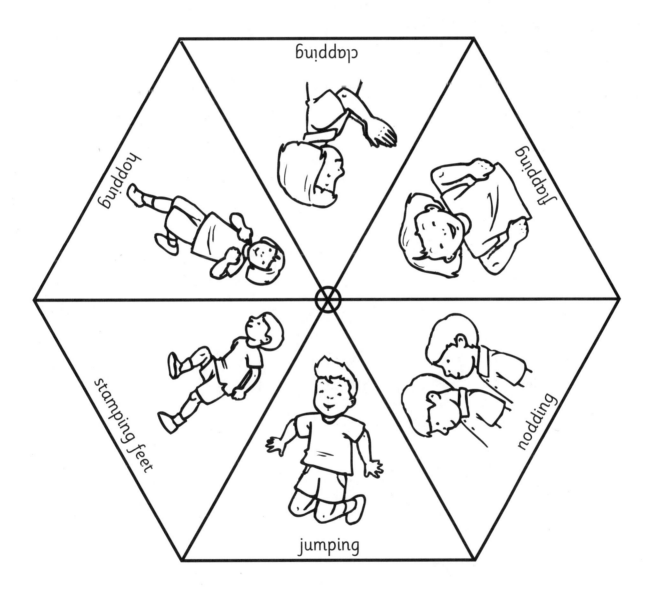

Bug cards

Photocopy on to card and cut out. Roll a dice with spots to indicate 1, 1, 2, 2, 3, 3 and ask which numbered card corresponds with the number rolled.

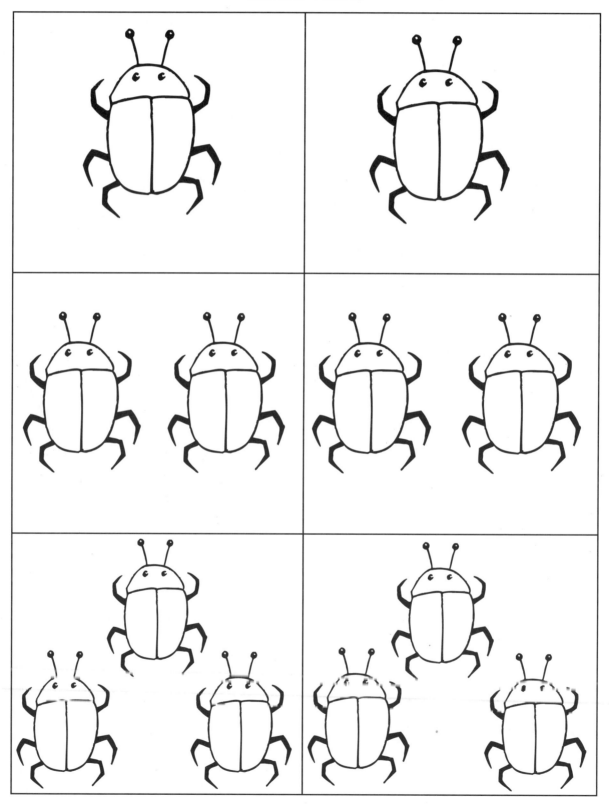

Number squares

Photocopy and help the children to cut out. Use as part of a tiddlywinks
game.

Flapjack

Cut out and fold along the dotted lines.

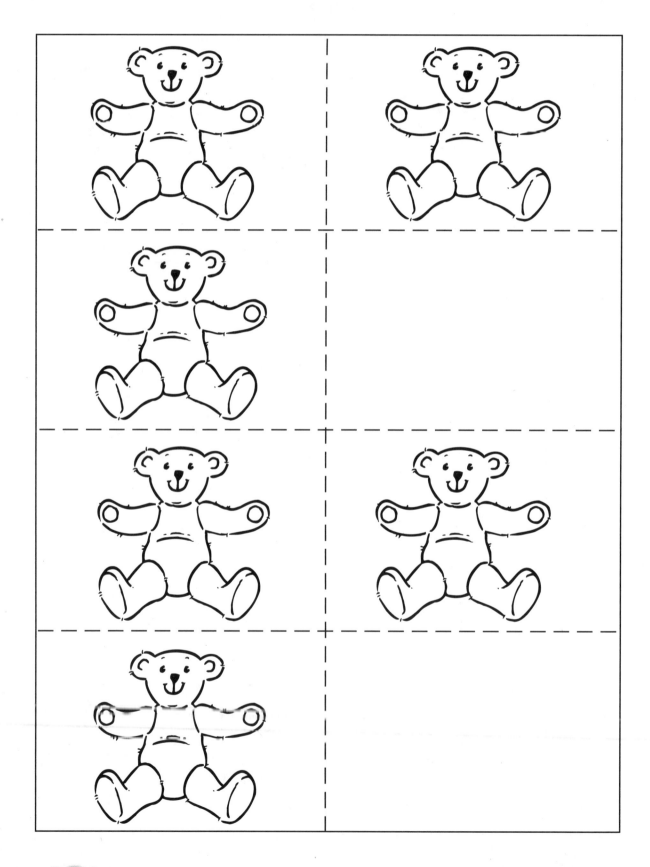

Bingo boards

1	6	3	3	2	1
5	4	2	4	6	5
1	4	3	5	2	6
2	6	5	4	1	3

Heads or tails?

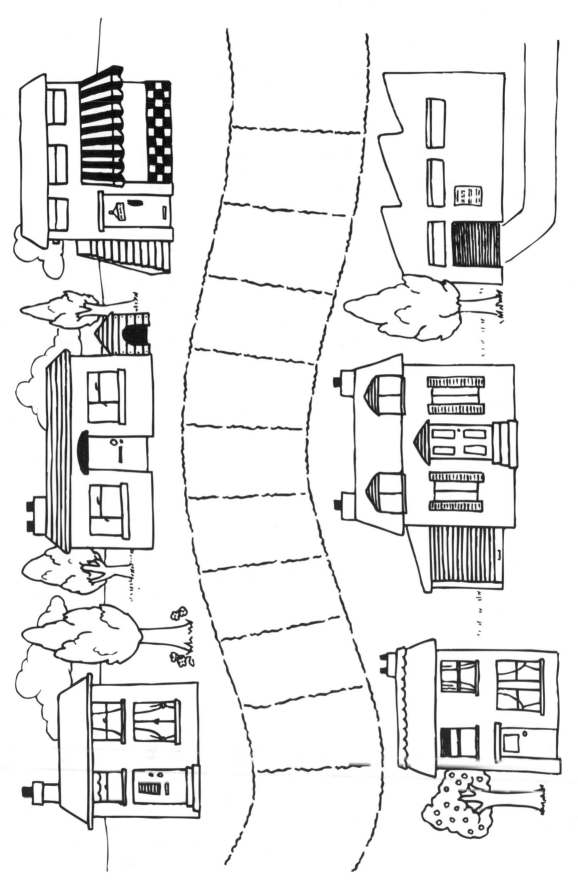

Mrs Wishy-Washy

(Tune: 'Here We Go Round the Mulberry Bush')

This is the way we wash our socks,
We wash our socks, we wash our socks.
This is the way we wash our socks,
And hang them out to dry.

How many socks are on the line?
On the line, on the line.
How many socks are on the line?
Can you help us count them?

How many blue socks on the line?
On the line, on the line.
How many blue socks on the line?
Can you help us count them?

How many short socks on the line?
On the line, on the line.
How many short socks on the line?
Can you help us count them?

How many stripy socks on the line?
On the line, on the line.
How many stripy socks on the line?
Can you help us count them?

Helen Elis Jones

Square dancing

See how this dance forms a square. Can you make a different shape?

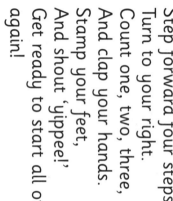

Step forward four steps,
Turn to your right.
Count one, two, three,
And clap your hands.
Stamp your feet,
And shout 'yippee!'
Get ready to start all over
again!

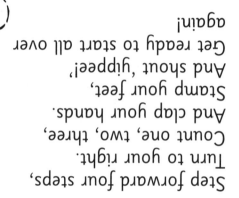

Step forward four steps,
Turn to your right.
Count one, two, three,
And clap your hands.
Stamp your feet,
And shout 'yippee!'
Get ready to start all over
again!

Step forward four steps,
Turn to your right.
Count one, two, three,
And clap your hands.
Stamp your feet,
And shout 'yippee!'
Get ready to start all over
again!

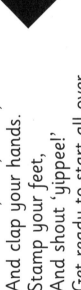

Step forward four steps,
Turn to your right.
Count one, two, three,
And clap your hands.
Stamp your feet,
And shout 'yippee!'
Get ready to start all over
again!

Teddies on the wall

Cut out along the solid outside line and in between each bear up to the dotted line. Use bottom portion to hold the wall.

Magic shapes

Cut out sections and fold along dotted line.

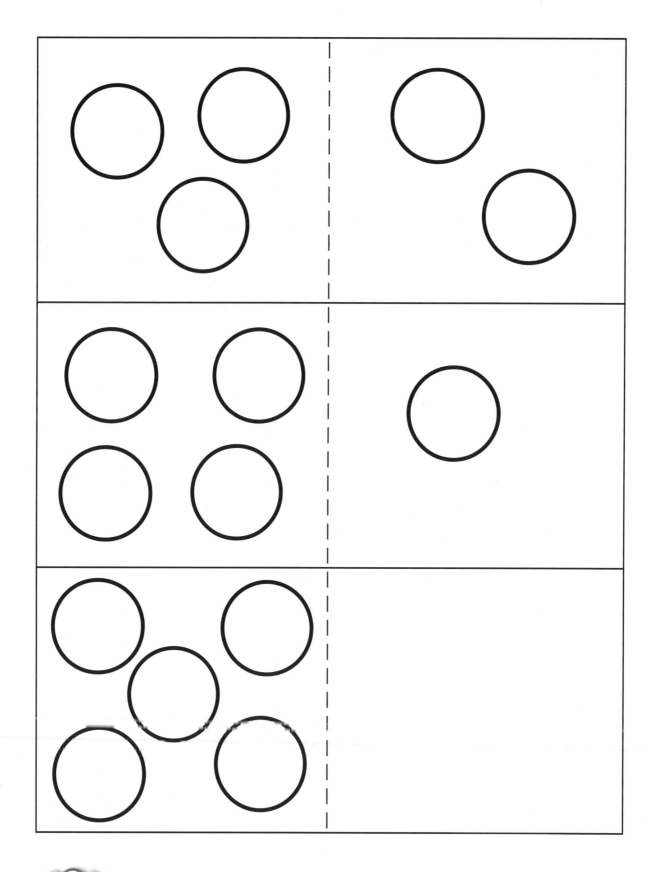

Teddy ruler

Using your five-bear ruler find objects which are...

shorter than five teddies	same size as five teddies	longer than five teddies

Lotto game

Cut out the top four shaped board. Use the lower one with older children.

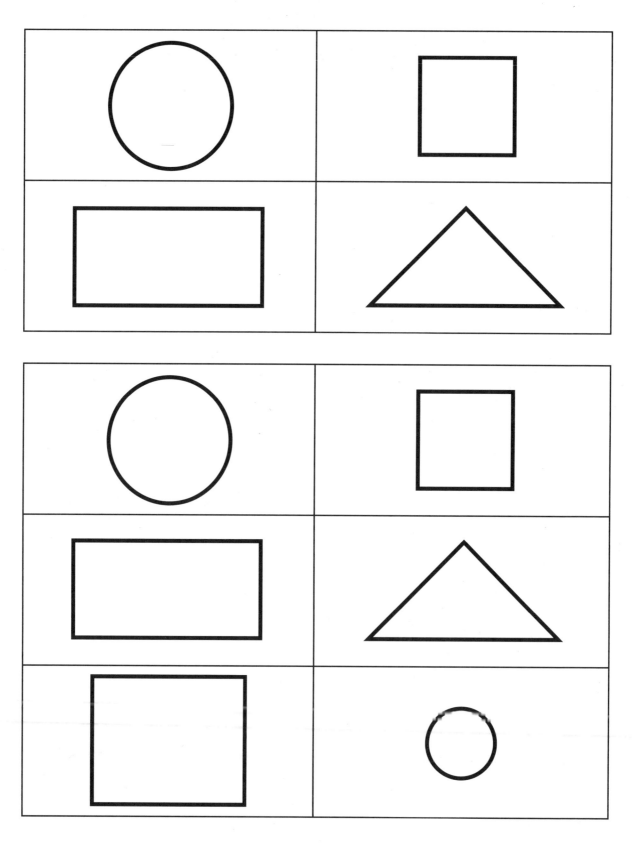

Folding stars

Photocopy, cut out and fold along the dotted lines.

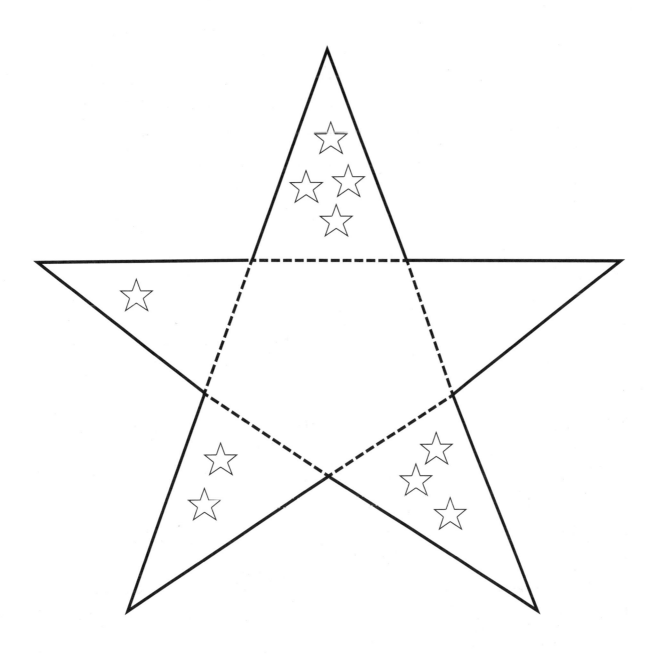

Shape labels

circle	triangle
square	rectangle
star	straight
curved	round
corner	face
side	edge
end	cube
pyramid	sphere
cone	roll
slide	flat